Old Testament Introduction 3
# THEOLOGY OF THE OLD TESTAMENT

**Formission**
Rowheath Pavilion
Heath Road
Bournville
FORMISSION  Birmingham B30 1HH

**TEF Study Guides**

This SPCK series was first sponsored by the Theological Education Fund of the WCC in response to requests from colleges in Africa, Asia, the Caribbean and South Pacific. The Guides continue to be written by and in consultation with theological tutors from all over the world, but have from the outset been as widely used by students and parish groups in the West as by those for whom English may be a second language. More advanced titles in the list are marked (A).

*General Editors*: Daphne Terry and Nicholas Beddow

IN PREPARATION

TEF Study Guide 15

Old Testament Introduction 3

# THEOLOGY OF THE OLD TESTAMENT

DAVID F. HINSON

First published in 1976
SPCK
Holy Trinity Church
Marylebone Road,
London NW1 4DU

Eighth impression 1992

## ACKNOWLEDGEMENTS

The photographs in this book are reproduced by
courtesy of the British Museum (p. 8), the Mansell
Collection, London (pp. 20, 83, 98, 113, 128, 134),
les Musées nationaux, Paris (p. 51),
Mr. A. F. Kersting (p. 57), Miss Sophia D. Lokko (p. 148a),
and Camera Press Ltd.

ISBN 0 281 02927 X
ISBN 0 281 02928 8 (special edition for Africa,
Asia, S. Pacific and Caribbean).

Printed and bound in Great Britain by
Hollen Street Press Ltd, Slough, Berks.

# Contents

# Illustrations and Charts

# Preface

Six years' work are now complete, and three Study Guides on the Old Testament are the result. Many people have worked together to enable me to prepare these volumes, and I shall always be grateful for their interest and support.

Miss D. Terry, Publications Secretary of the Theological Education Fund, not only invited me to write these books, but supported me throughout with advice and assistance of a very high editorial standard. Various secretaries have played their part, and I am this time particularly grateful to Miss Burnside and Mrs Tabak for typing the revised manuscript. The S.P.C.K. have presented all three volumes in a fashion pleasant to handle, and easy to refer to.

The Reverend Samuel Amirtham of Tamil Nadu Theological Seminary in South India commented on the proposed outline of this volume, and the original draft of the manuscript was examined in detail by my old friend and colleague, W. Vernon Stone, who is well aware of the needs of students who use English as a second language. Dr R. J. Coggins of King's College, London, has again given much scholarly guidance and advice without which I would not have dared to present the manuscript for publication. I have, of course, reserved the right to use my own judgement in what should be included in this volume, and any lack of balance or direct mistakes are entirely my own fault, for which I apologize.

The Methodist Church in Hemel Hempstead has employed me throughout the six years, and has allowed me time, especially in the summer months, for the work of preparing these books. I have received nothing but friendship and encouragement from those in authority, and many of my people have expressed their interest in this contribution to the life of the World Church.

Last but by no means least, my own family has given me support throughout, even though it has meant that I have not always been free to relax and enjoy leisure when they have been available to share time with me. Betty, my wife, has given continual interest and encouragement, and Peter and Mary have grown up to be introduced to the Old Testament through these books, showing a real interest in them. They have all been a real blessing to me.

May this book serve to encourage others to take up or continue the study of the Old Testament and discover its message for today.

*Hemel Hempstead*                                                    DAVID F. HINSON

# Using this Book

This is the third book in a three-volume course on the Old Testament. The first volume was about the history of Israel, and the development of Jewish religious practices. The second volume was about the books of the Old Testament. The studies included in those two volumes were a necessary preparation for the study in this volume of the Theology of the Old Testament.

Readers will not fully understand this subject and what is written in this volume without a proper knowledge of the subjects already dealt with in the earlier books of this course. Some students may not have used the first two volumes, but provided they have studied the subjects in some other way, they will be ready to begin work on the Theology of the Old Testament.

### WHAT IS OLD TESTAMENT THEOLOGY?

It is all that God revealed about Himself, about mankind, and about the world, which is contained in the books of the Old Testament. It is not identical with New Testament Theology, because in the times when these books were written and edited Christ had not yet come. All that happened in Old Testament times was a preparation for the coming of Christ. People began to understand something about the nature of God, and to experience fellowship with Him. Their minds and hearts were prepared by those experiences, and those insights, so that when Christ came they could understand who He was, and what He was doing for mankind. When we study Old Testament Theology we are sharing in that preparation for the coming of Christ, by thinking about the things which the people of Old Testament times learnt about God and His purposes.

### DO WE NEED TO STUDY OLD TESTAMENT THEOLOGY?

Some people say that because Christ has come we have the full revelation of God in the writings of the New Testament, and can go straight to them without needing to study the Old Testament. Some among them say that there is a sufficient preparation for understanding Christ in the things that their own tribe or nation have discovered about God, as it is taught in the traditional religion of their people. They say that the Old Testament was a preparation for the coming of Christ in Israel, but that Animism, Hinduism, Buddhism, or whatever other religion is practised in their country, is the preparation for Christ among their own people.

This sort of argument does draw our attention to the fact that God did not limit Himself to working among one people, the Israelites. He has always been working to make Himself known to all people in every place. Some of the insights and understandings of the non-biblical religions can be seen to be the result of God's inspiration. Paul recognized this fact: Romans 1.19. John wrote about it in the prologue to his Gospel : John 1.9.

It also reminds us that everyone begins thinking about theological issues in the light of ideas that are current among their own people: whether these ideas are biblical or not. Each person has to weigh and consider the thoughts about God that he has been taught from childhood, or that are offered to him as an adult. He needs to do so to discover whether they give him an adequate basis for faith and life. He will quickly appreciate those parts of the Bible which deal with matters that he has already given thought to, especially if they seem to provide him with a better understanding of the matter which he has been considering. Since Christ is right at the centre of the revelation of God, most people will appreciate the appeal of the Gospels before they come to understand and value other parts of the Bible. They will see in Jesus the riches of revelation which are available to them as they search for an understanding of life.

But Christians should not remain content to see only that part of God's revelation which is most obvious and appealing to them because it relates to the particular issues which interest them as a result of their earlier searches for religious truth. We have a responsibility to search out the fullest details of the revelation contained in the New Testament, and so to know Christ in all His glory. When we begin to study the New Testament with a determination to understand it fully, we quickly discover that we need to know what preceded it in the life of the People of Israel. Then the study of Old Testament Theology becomes highly relevant and full of meaning for us. In the light of this study we come to know Christ more closely, and to benefit more fully from God's revelation.

## BIBLE VERSION

The English translation of the Bible used and quoted in this Study Guide is the Common Bible edition of the Revised Standard Version. This version is referred to as the RSV in this volume. The abbreviations used in this Guide for the titles of the books of the Bible are the same as those listed at the front of the RSV, except for the following: Exodus (Exod.), Isaiah (Isa.) and Matthew (Matt.).

READING THIS GUIDE

In this volume there are a large number of Bible references drawn from many part of the Old Testament. It will be found helpful to read each section of the Guide straight through once to get the general sense, without referring to the Bible itself, and then to read sentence by sentence looking up all the Bible references. Notice especially how the same or similar ideas are found in different parts of the Old Testament. Try to remember the date of the preparation of each book mentioned, and compare what is said in the Torah, the Prophets, and the Writings.

STUDY SUGGESTIONS

Suggestions for further study and revision appear at the end of each section. They are intended to help readers to study more thoroughly, and to relate what they have read to the ideas held by the people amongst whom they live. It is best to try to answer these questions without referring back to what has been read in the section on which the exercise is based. A good English dictionary (e.g. *The Advanced Learner's Dictionary of Current English*, published by Oxford University Press), and a complete Concordance, are essential tools for this work. A Bible Dictionary, and an Atlas of the Bible lands may also help.

The *Key to Study Suggestions* is given on pp. 151–160. Only occasionally is a complete answer given there. More often the Key shows where an answer may be found within the chapters of this Guide. Some questions depend on local circumstances, and no exact answer can be given in the Key, or they are questions for discussion and debate.

ILLUSTRATIONS

The photographs in this volume serve two separate purposes. Some illustrate the ideas that were current among other peoples in the times of the Old Testament, and compare or contrast them with what the Jews believed. Others relate Old Testament ideas to the world of today, and encourage us to recognize the relevance of what we read.

THE INDEXES

Two Indexes are provided. *The Subject Index* (pp. 173–176) includes all the major subjects mentioned in the Guide; but only the major references to each subject are listed, so that the Index is a guide to the most important thoughts on each subject. *The Bible Reference Index* (pp. 161–171) is much fuller and longer than in the earlier volumes because it is not possible to group the references to a particular book of the Old Testament. References to some of the books are scattered widely throughout the Guide, indicating the breadth of the theological teaching they contain.

# Further Reading

Readers may find the following books useful for further study of Old Testament Theology. Some of these titles are intended for the more advanced student.

Bailey, L. R., *Biblical Perspectives on Death*. Fortress Press 1979.
Campbell, D. B. J., *The Old Testament for Modern Readers*. John Murray 1972.
Dyrness, W., *Themes in Old Testament Theology*. Paternoster Press 1980.
Edwards, D., *Key to the Old Testament*. Collins 1976.
Jones, E., *God, Man and the Community*.
Knight, G. A. F., *I am: This is My Name*. Eerdmans 1983.
Myers, J. M., *Grace and the Torah*. Fortress Press 1975.
Sawyer, F. A., *From Moses to Patmos*. SPCK 1977.
Westermann, C., *What does the Old Testament say about God?* SPCK 1979.
Wood, L. J., *The Holy Spirit in the Old Testament*. Zondervan 1976.

# Introduction: The Word of God

## THE OLD TESTAMENT AS THE WORD OF GOD

Some people read the Old Testament because it contains beautiful poetry and exciting stories. Others read it because the Old Testament helps to complete their knowledge of the history of mankind. But most people who read it do so because they believe the Old Testament is part of the Word of God. As Christians we value the Old Testament because it helps us to understand the character and purpose of God, and the nature and destiny of mankind.

This third volume in our course in the Old Testament is concerned with this understanding of God and man. We shall study what the Old Testament has to teach us, and how it helps us to have a living relationship with God and to share in the fulfilment of His purposes for us.

We must begin, however, by being clear in our own minds what we mean when we say that the Old Testament is 'the Word of God'. We shall only begin to understand what the Old Testament teaches, if we first consider how its message is presented to us.

Christians have different ideas about the meaning of the phrase 'The Word of God'. Part of the problem is a grammatical difficulty. The little word *of* can carry more than one meaning. Think about the following sentence: 'You can trust the word of an honest man.' Here the word *of* could be replaced by the phrase 'spoken by' without changing the meaning of the sentence. But now notice this sentence: 'Have you had word of Mr Smith since last we met?' Here *of* could be replaced by 'about'. The questioner wants to know if there is any news *about* Mr Smith. Which meaning for the word *of* is the correct one in the phrase 'the Word of God'? Some Christians take it to mean 'the Word spoken by God'; and others prefer to interpret the phrase as 'the Word about God'. We shall see later that there is another interpretation which is probably more helpful than either of these, but let us now consider these two ideas about the Old Testament.

### I. 'THE WORD SPOKEN BY GOD'

It would be very easy for us to understand and accept the teaching of the Old Testament if we could be assured that the whole of Scripture is a record of 'the Word spoken by God'. We believe that God is always honest; so we could turn to any chapter and any verse and find

1

something that God said, which we would accept as true. Some Christians use the Old Testament in this way. They accept without question everything that they read in it. If anything they read seems puzzling to understand, or difficult to accept, they blame themselves for failing to appreciate what is written. They feel distrustful of any attempts to explain the difficulties as arising from the inaccuracies and misunderstandings of human authors and copyists.

It is a fact that as we turn the pages of the Old Testament we do find words which are recorded as having been spoken by God. In Genesis 1 the phrase 'God said' occurs ten times, each time followed by a command of God which led to a further stage in the creation of the world. Again, one of the most frequent phrases to be found in the prophetic books is 'thus says the LORD' (Amos 1.3, 6, 9, etc.). But there is no real doubt that human writers have recorded these things, and have produced the books that we read in the Old Testament.

Many of the words and sentences in the Old Testament are not words recorded as spoken by God Himself. Sometimes we know who spoke what we read—especially in the legends and history recorded in the Old Testament. We can read the words of Abraham (Gen. 13.8, 9, etc.), Moses (Exod. 4.1, etc.), and David (1 Sam. 20.1). But we do not know the names of the writers who recorded the stories of these men, and we cannot be sure how far they were recording remembered sayings, and how far they invented suitable sayings to complete the stories that they were retelling. Sometimes we do not even know who first used the words we read, but we can see that they express the thoughts of some ancient writer about God, e.g. Psalms 92, 121, etc. These are not words spoken by God Himself.

We need to remember that the Old Testament is a human document. It was written by men, and it records their experiences and expresses their faith in God.

## 2. 'THE WORD ABOUT GOD'

Anybody who turns the pages of the Old Testament will quickly realize that in the Bible there is much which is written about God. Even a man who denies that God exists cannot deny that the Old Testament is *about* God. All he can say is that those who helped to write the Old Testament believed in God, and tried to explain life and history by using the idea of God. Such a man will deny that the writers have given an accurate account of events, because he does not believe in God and cannot accept a presentation of history which is based on belief in God.

It is important for us to realize that the people who wrote the Old Testament did so because they had shared in some experience of life which convinced them that God was a living reality. They felt that they must pass on to others the things which had convinced them of His reality. For some of them it was the whole history of their people up to their own day which convinced them that God had a plan of salvation for Israel. For others it was the wisdom and the justice of the laws handed down to them from earlier generations which convinced them of the rule of God. For the prophets, a more personal experience drove them to try to interpret the events of their own day in the light of God's rule, and of His purpose for His people. For the Psalmists, it was the sense of God's presence and power in the midst of a worshipping congregation which inspired them to write about the glories of God. For the wise-men of Old Testament days it was the intellectual struggles and the sudden gleams of new light on their problems which led them to record the truth about life as they then saw it. They were all writing about God, convinced of the truth of what they wrote.

Anybody who reads the Bible must come to a decision about the value of these writings. As we have seen, people who deny the existence of God will treat the Old Testament at best as an interesting record of the ideas of the people of ancient Israel. They will not accept that these ideas are true. But those who have some experience of God, and believe that He does reveal Himself to people, will be glad to read of the experiences of others, and will compare their own discoveries in the spiritual world with those of the people of ancient Israel. They will find much which matches their own experience of God, but some of the ideas expressed in the Old Testament will seem to conflict with their own experience of God. They will want to understand why the people of Israel believed as they did in these matters, but will probably prefer to read and re-read those parts of the Old Testament which confirm their own experiences.

But this is not a complete answer to our question about the way in which the Old Testament is part of 'The Word of God', because it leaves us to judge for ourselves what is true and what is less than the truth. It suggests that a person's own judgement of spiritual reality is the best guide to eternal truth. But the Church has always recognized that the Bible has an authority for Christians, and that truth comes to us from the Bible in fresh and convincing ways. Does the phrase 'the Word of God' then mean more than 'the Word about God'?

### 3. 'THE WORD THAT BELONGS TO GOD'
The word *of* has as its simplest meaning: 'belonging to', i.e. it expresses the idea that a thing is for use by, and under the control of, its owner. The flag *of* Zambia, for example, is for use by the people of Zambia, and is under their control. Nobody else can use it properly unless with the permission and by the direction of the government and people of Zambia. Let us explore this idea as it relates to the Old Testament, which is the word *of* God.

The Old Testament is for God's use, and He controls its right use. We shall understand its proper value and significance as we come to understand God's ways and God's purposes. We shall fail to understand the Old Testament aright if we forget that God was involved in its preparation, and that the human experience which it expresses springs from God's activity among men. The basic truth is that, from the very beginning, God planned for, and worked for, the day when human beings would have a personal living relationship with Him, through which they would come to understand His greatness and glory. The Bible came into being as a human response to this divine activity. It was preserved as a means by which people could share together the knowledge of God that came from this activity of His.

So the Bible has come into being as a result of the meeting of God with men, and men with God. The ways in which this meeting happens are usually described by the two words 'inspiration' and 'revelation'. These words refer to different aspects of God's relationship with men.

*Inspiration* is the process by which God stimulates people to think fresh thoughts, and to seek new understanding. He does this in many different ways, but always people must be willing to respond and to search out the significance of their new experience of God. Otherwise they do not gain the full benefit of His activity.

*Revelation* is the process by which God actually gives people new knowledge and new understanding. It is the proper result of inspiration. People must be willing to grasp and accept and use the new knowledge, if the process of revelation is to reach its fulfilment. They must make their new knowledge a real foundation for life and activity, and especially for their relationship with God Himself.

These two processes of inspiration and revelation can be recognized in all events and experiences described in the Old Testament. Those who wrote the Old Testament were expressing their own individual response to the activity of God. They were experiencing the prompting of God's spirit in the inspiration which made them search out new truth from all that was happening to them, and to their nation. They were grappling with the truth which God was revealing, and they were seeking to express it in ways which their fellow Israelites would understand and appreciate.

Each generation of writers were men of their own time, who had shared in the benefits of God's work among His people in earlier periods. God was able to lead them on to fresh discoveries and new understanding, which they in turn shared with those who came after them. So, as the centuries passed, there grew up a great fund of knowledge of God and of His purposes. And this provided the opportunity for deeper understanding and richer experience of fellowship with God for succeeding generations.

4

Eventually the time was right for the coming of Christ. Those who accepted and lived by the truth which men of earlier centuries had recorded for them, were able to share in the new revelation which came into the world full and complete in Jesus Christ. All that the Old Testament recorded was a necessary preparation to enable men and women to respond to the grace and truth that was in Him (John 1.17).

In a similar way, the Old Testament can prepare us today, by helping to deepen and enrich our spiritual understanding. It can enable us to appreciate more fully the person and work of Christ, and make us alert to, and ready for, God's presence and activity in our own lives, and in our own communities. The Old Testament is the Word of God for us because it enables us to draw close to God and know His living presence, and to share fellowship with Him in common with other believers. This is the purpose for which it was written: that we and all generations might be inspired and led into a personal relationship with, and knowledge of, God.

## STUDY SUGGESTIONS

WORDS

1. Make up sentences of your own using the word 'of' in each of the three senses used in this chapter: i.e. (a) 'spoken by', (b) 'about', (c) 'belonging to'.
2. The word 'Word' can be used in several different ways. Which two of the following terms come nearest to the meaning of 'Word' in the phrase 'Word of God'?
   command   communication   information   intercourse   promise
   proverb   report   statement   vow

CONTENT

3. In what senses is the Old Testament a 'human document'? Give examples to illustrate your answer.
4. (a) What is the difference between Revelation and Inspiration?
   (b) What is man's part in each of these experiences?
5. What is the importance of reading about other people's experiences of God?

BIBLE

6. Use a Concordance to study the way in which the writers of the New Testament use the words 'reveal', and 'revelation'.
   (a) Do they give most emphasis to past experiences of divine revelation, or do they regard it as a present and future experience?
   (b) In what way does their use of the words affect our understanding of the nature and significance of revelation.

DISCUSSION

7. (a) When the prophets use the words 'Thus says the LORD', what do they mean?

(b) Which of the following alternatives expresses most clearly the truth of their experiences?

(i) 'I have heard the audible voice of God and now pass on His exact words to you.'

(ii) 'Because I have clear ideas of what God is like, I think that this is what He would say in the present circumstances.'

(iii) 'God has given me an insight into His purpose and I am now trying to share this insight with you.'

8. (a) When we read the Old Testament, what do we expect to find:

(i) Precise theological statements about God and his purpose?

(ii) Men's attempts to express what they have experienced of God in the circumstances of their daily life?

(iii) Promises and prophecies made by God, and recorded word for word by men?

(iv) Anything else?

(b) How will what we expect to find influence our understanding of what we read?

Use the following passages to illustrate your answer: Exodus 21.15–17; Amos 9.2–4; Job 27.1–6.


## GOD'S WORK OF INSPIRATION

We have seen that, according to the writers of the Old Testament, God has always been at work in people's lives in order to establish a personal fellowship, a living relationship with them. This new life that He has been offering involves people in new thoughts, new feelings, and new activities. 'Inspiration' is the name we give to the process by which God stimulates us towards these new ways of living. By inspiration He challenges us to live the sort of life which is a freely chosen response to Him, and to His plans and purposes for mankind.

We need now to take a closer look at the ways in which God inspired people in Old Testament times to live as His servants, and to do His will. The writers of the Old Testament describe many of the experiences which made the great men of those days think and feel and act as they did. These descriptions help us to see God at work inspiring men to new life.

It will help us to understand our own experiences of God if we examine the means of inspiration described in the Old Testament. We should not, however, expect to share in every one of these sorts of experience. They are tools for God's work, and are under His control. He knows how best to bring inspiration to each of us, and to the Christian communities to which we belong. We need only to be alert to the ways in which God approaches people, so that we may recognize the times when He draws near to us.

## 1. DREAMS

Many of the great men of Old Testament times are described as receiving inspiration through dreams. Jacob knew through a dream that God would be with him in his travels (Gen. 28.12–15). Joseph learnt through his dreams that he was to be a leader of men (Gen. 37.5–11). Solomon was promised wisdom in a dream (1 Kings 3.4–15). In the Gospels Joseph and the wise men received warnings of danger through dreams (Matt. 2.12, 13). The gift of the Holy Spirit at the time of the new age would result in further significant dreams (Joel 2.28; and compare Acts 2.17).

However, there are clear warnings in the Old Testament about false dreams, and about people who tell others of false dreams as though they were genuine messages from God (Deut. 13.1–5; Jer. 23.32; Zech. 10.2). God alone can provide the right interpretation for dreams, and it is those who live in close fellowship with Him who can discern the truth (Gen. 40.8).

## 2. VISIONS

A vision is similar in many ways to a dream, except that it comes to people when they are awake and alert, and does not depend upon the relaxation of sleep. Moses probably saw a vision when 'the angel of the LORD appeared to him in a flame of fire out of the midst of a bush' (Exod. 3.2). The disciple of Elisha saw a vision of 'horses and chariots of fire' protecting the prophet from his enemies (2 Kings 6.17). Isaiah saw a vision of seraphim, and one of them touching his lips with a burning coal (Isa. 6.6,7). Ezekiel saw a vision of God as a human figure surrounded by fire (Ezek. 1.26–28).

The Old Testament also contains warnings about paying attention to false visions. Some men are said to describe 'visions of their own minds, not from the mouth of the LORD' (Jer. 23.16). Some priests and prophets 'err in vision, they stumble in giving judgement' (Isa. 28.7). But when the Holy Spirit is poured out on all men, 'young men shall see visions' (Joel 2.28).

## 3. SIGNS

Often in giving visions God takes up and uses natural and ordinary things, and includes them in the mysterious experience. There was a bush that was the starting point of the vision of Moses. The temple and the smoke of sacrifices helped to provide the material for Isaiah's vision. But sometimes men were quickened by God to recognize

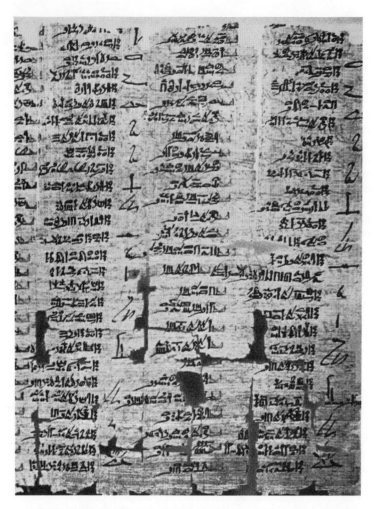

Throughout human history people have been interested in dreams, and have wanted to interpret them. This is part of an Egyptian papyrus from about 1300 BC which suggests explanations for some of the things seen in dreams, e.g.: 'If a man sees himself in a dream (a) plunging into the river—good: it means cleansing from all evils . . . (b) seeing his face in a mirror—bad: it means another wife.'

Biblical writers believed that 'God alone can provide the right interpretation for dreams' (p. 7). What do your own people think about dreams? What do *you* think?

spiritual truth as a result of seeing quite ordinary sights. Amos saw a plumb-line set against a wall, and it revealed to him God's intention to judge Israel (Amos 7.7–9). The plumb-line became a sign for Amos, and later he described its effect upon him, as he preached to others. Similarly Jeremiah saw a boiling pot tilting over, and it became a sign to him of God's judgement of Judah (Jer. 1.13).

Sometimes the priests or prophets set up particular objects as permanent reminders to the people of what God had done. Joshua set up an altar near the Jordan as a sign (Josh. 4.6, 7). It served to remind them of God's ways with Israel, and so prepared their hearts for His coming. Sometimes a future event was promised in God's name, and the fulfilment of the promise would be a sign of His power and mercy (1 Sam. 10.2–10; 2 Kings 19.29, etc.).

But signs could be misinterpreted by the prophets, and the Israelites were warned to be on guard against those who supported false teaching with signs, even if the signs were fulfilled (Deut. 13.1–5). Jeremiah 27—28 records a dispute between Jeremiah and Hananiah over the meaning of a yoke which Jeremiah wore. Each of them claimed to know the interpretation of the sign, even though they expressed opposite ideas. At the end of the argument Jeremiah explained the difference between them: 'the LORD has not sent you' (Jer. 28.15).

### 4. MIRACLES

The word 'miracles' seldom appears in the Old Testament. Men preferrred to use a word which is best translated 'wonder'. This term expresses the special character of a miracle. It is something which makes people wonder. It is an event or an experience which we cannot explain in the way that we normally explain natural events.

Usually Old Testament writers describe such things as being the direct result of God's activity in the world. Perhaps some of them used this interpretation too quickly and too easily, without considering the possibility of a natural explanation. When we read what they wrote, we may feel compelled to question their judgement of an event, and to suggest some other cause for it, as we have done at times in Volume 1 of this course. Even so, unexpected, apparently unnatural, and unexplained events and experiences gave people a lively sense of God's presence and power, and this was a starting point for a deepening relationship with Him. For example, when the Israelites followed a pillar of cloud by day, and a pillar of fire by night, it may have been an erupting volcano which they could see far away towards the East (Exod. 13.21). But if so, God was using it for His own purposes, and the Israelites were right to believe that He wanted them to regard it as a sign to guide their travels. By this thing God was preparing them for their experiences at Mount Sinai.

## 5. THE WORDS OF MEN

The Old Testament described many occasions when God challenged
and inspired people most clearly and directly through the words of
their fellows. Samuel, for example, was called to be God's messenger
to Eli and to the Israelites. Samuel was personally alert and aware of the
presence of God, and so he was able to express to others God's purposes
for His people (1 Sam. 3.10–14). The law-givers, the kings, the priests,
the prophets, and the collectors of wisdom all served at one time or
another as spokesmen for God. Their words challenged individuals or
the community to seek new ways of life which would bring them nearer
to God. These men were a source of inspiration to their fellows,
opening up the way to fellowship with God. Yet none of these human
spokesmen escaped entirely from the accusation that they were using
their authority in false and misleading ways.

None of these experiences by which God quickened men to a sense
of his presence and power was enough by itself to provide a full and
complete guide to the religious life. Each could be misunderstood by
people who were not willing to receive new truth. Each could be
misinterpreted by leaders who did not want the people to know what
God was saying. Yet through these varied sorts of experience God could
and did draw near to people, and offer them a living fellowship with
Himself. His ultimate purpose was that they should know Him for
themselves. 'No longer shall each man teach his neighbour and each
his brother, saying "Know the LORD", for they shall all know me,
from the least of them to the greatest, says the LORD: for I will forgive
their iniquity, and I will remember their sin no more' (Jer. 31.34).

# STUDY SUGGESTIONS

### WORDS

1. Which three of the following words are nearest in meaning to the
   word 'inspiration', as it is used in this chapter?
   discernment    dramatization    encouragement    originality
   prompting    sensation    stimulus
2. Which *two* of the following words could be used to describe the
   dreams and the visions of inspired men?
   concrete    delusion    fanciful    imaginary    instructive

### CONTENT

3. Describe in your own words the difference between *visions* and *signs*
   in the Old Testament.
4. (a) Which offices held by the leaders of Israel involved them in
   being spokesmen for God?

(b) Did those who held these offices always serve well as God's spokesmen?

Give examples, with chapter and verse references, to support your answer.

BIBLE

5. The word 'inspiration' is not found in the RSV Old Testament. Instead, the idea is expressed by describing the activity of the Spirit of the LORD. Use a Concordance to study the verses in Ezekiel in which this Spirit is mentioned. Summarize what is said in that book about the influence of God's Spirit upon the prophet.

6. 'By inspiration God challenges us to live the sort of life which is a freely chosen response to Him, and to His plans and purposes for mankind' (p. 6).

Show that the writers of the Old Testament believed that it was possible to reject inspiration. Collect as many verses as you can in which men are described as having rejected God and His purposes.

DISCUSSION

7. Miracles are described in this chapter as 'unexpected, apparently unnatural, and unexplained events and experiences'.

(a) Do you think this is an adequate description, or would you want to qualify it in any way?

(b) What difference, if any, does it make that we are sometimes able to give natural explanations of what happened?

8. 'All the various ways by which God drew near to men in Old Testament times could be misinterpreted by leaders who did not want the people to know what God was saying.'

In what way, if any, could the people of Israel recognize those who were truly inspired, and distinguish them from those who were not?

9. (a) How do we today become aware of the presence and power of God in our own lives, and in the life of the community in which we live?

(b) In what ways does knowledge of the experiences of people in Old Testament times help us to appreciate and understand our own experiences?


## GOD'S WORK OF REVELATION

We have seen that inspiration is the process by which God draws near to men, and calls them into fellowship with Himself. Through the experience of God we gain new knowledge about His character and purposes, and the possibility of new ways of life. The processes of

11

giving and receiving this new knowledge are both part of what we call 'revelation'. God gives and man receives, and both these activities must take place before revelation is complete.

Through our knowledge of Jesus we know what God is like: 'the same yesterday and today and for ever' (Heb. 13.8). His character does not change: He is for ever perfect (Matt. 5.48). His purposes do not change (Eph. 3.11). God's activities in relationship with men only change according to the needs of the situation, in order to achieve His eternal purposes (Jer. 18.5–11). What God has revealed through all the ages is Truth about Himself and His purposes—the same Truth which God seeks to make known to all men. This Truth can be expressed in many different ways in many different situations. But, rightly understood, all that we know about God and His purposes fits together as one pattern of Truth, to be distinguished from all that is false.

But no one person can claim to have a mastery of the whole Truth about God. Each receives some part of the Truth through his own experience of God. We each benefit by sharing in the experience and knowledge of others who also serve the LORD. As we share our knowledge together, we come nearer to appreciating the whole Truth which is in the heart and mind of God. The books of the Bible themselves were written as a way for men to share together their knowledge of God. We reach out towards the Truth as we share and appreciate the experiences of those who wrote the Bible.

God responds to our search for the Truth by leading us into deeper understanding. He is the perfect teacher: He knows best what we need to learn, and He knows best the ways in which we can learn. God does not teach us by providing us with an accurate factual statement of the realities of the situation, for statements are easily misunderstood, and the Truth cannot be confined to a few words. Statements and words always have associations with the experiences and understanding of the people of any particular generation, and are seldom adequate to express what is important to later generations, for whom they may mean something different.

Instead, God encourages us to think for ourselves, and gradually He opens up the way for us through new experiences towards deeper appreciation and a fuller knowledge of the Truth. Any teacher knows that this is the creative and effective way to tackle the responsibility. God is the great example on which all teachers should model their work.

We can see evidence of God's work as a teacher in the experiences which are described in the Old Testament. We need to be aware of the pattern of His work, in order to understand for ourselves the Truth that is in the Old Testament. Let us take notice of some of the things which every good teacher knows to be important, and see how the Bible shows us God using these methods.

'God opens up the way for us through new experiences towards deeper appreciation and fuller knowledge of the Truth' (p. 12).

The experience of space travel gave the astronauts Borman, Lovell, and Anders a deeper awareness of God's greatness, and they witnessed to this revelation by broadcasting passages from the Bible as their spacecraft Apollo 8 orbited the moon. A woman belonging to a Zionist Church in Southern Africa experiences the spirit of power, and is inspired to 'speak in tongues' while the ministers pray beside her.

Through what experiences, if any, have you been aware of God's revelation or inspiration?

1. 'START FROM WHERE THE STUDENTS ARE: BUILD NEW KNOW-
LEDGE ON WHAT THEY KNOW ALREADY'

The religion of the Patriarchs was closely related to Animism, the belief in 'spirits' on which many peoples still base their religion today. Their religious experiences were closely related to natural objects, which in Animism are thought to be inhabited by spirits: e.g. trees (Gen. 18.1), stones (Gen. 28.11), streams (Gen. 32.22–32), and mountains (Exod. 19.16, 17). The early Israelites expected spiritual experiences in such places, and God used their expectations as the starting point for new experiences, and new knowledge. They did not meet spirits, they met God. So they left Animism behind them, because it was an inadequate explanation of their experiences.

2. 'WORK IN A WELL-PLANNED ORDER: SOME THINGS MUST BE
LEARNT BEFORE OTHERS CAN BE UNDERSTOOD'

Christians are often puzzled by the fact that the writers of the Old Testament seem to have very little idea of the Trinity of God: Father, Son, and Holy Spirit. But the Israelites lived at a time when most of the neighbouring nations believed in many different gods. The most important idea in the religious education of the Jews was that God is One. It was only when they had fully grasped the idea of the Unity of God, with all that it implies, that they were ready to receive the Truth of the Trinity: the Three-in-One. Jesus came, and men learnt this Truth out of their experience of him. The Old Testament shows how people's understanding of other truths about God also developed only gradually. For example, the knowledge of God's justice was necessary before people could fully understand his mercy.

3. 'TAKE ACCOUNT OF VARYING ABILITY IN THE CLASS'

In any class some students will understand more quickly than others. They will not all make progress at the same speed. The wise teacher is able to stimulate and inspire the brightest student, and at the same time encourage the slowest. At any time in the history of Israel there were a few men who were outstanding in their spiritual understanding. They were far ahead of their own generation. Others held on to outworn ideas, and failed to appreciate the new measure of Truth available at their time.

Some scholars have tried to see in the Old Testament a clear pattern of development in understanding, and have assumed that all the Israelites developed in understanding at the same speed. They argue, for example, that Moses could not have believed that there was only one God, since there were people of his and later generations who still believed in many. But it seems more likely that the ordinary people took a longer time to reach the level of understanding which Moses had achieved much sooner. Often in history there have been pioneers of new knowledge who have been well ahead of the people of their day: Moses was one of these.

4. 'TEACH BY PUTTING STUDENTS INTO SITUATIONS WHERE THEIR KNOWLEDGE IS NECESSARY'

The practical use of theoretical knowledge is the best way to master a new truth. For example, if you want to learn a language, the best way is to go where you will need to use it in order to be understood. Then your knowledge will be important to you, and will become more firmly fixed in your mind through use. The Bible shows God using this method. He did not lead His people away from places of conflict and trouble so as to leave them free to think and study as the way to master new truth. He brought them to a land which has been a centre of conflict all through the centuries. They had to learn from experience that God controls all history, and they had to struggle with this truth in the middle of international conflict. As a result, they came to a new appreciation of what it means to be God's people, and of how God works out His purposes among men. They reached a new understanding of the meaning and purpose of suffering, first as a refining fire, and later as a means for the redemption of sinners.

## THE THEOLOGY OF THE OLD TESTAMENT

The importance of the Old Testament is that it is a record of God's work of revelation, making Himself known to the people of Israel so that they could be prepared to receive Jesus Christ as the One sent by God to fulfil His purposes on earth, and among men. When we ask: 'What did God teach His people in Old Testament times?' we are asking to know what is contained in the Theology of the Old Testament. This whole volume is written to help you discover the answer to this question.

We are not merely concerned to discover what the Patriarchs believed —or the people of David's time, or those who lived in exile. That is the study of Old Testament Religion. We have spent time thinking about that in Volume 1 of this course, in the third section of each chapter.

Nor are we merely concerned to notice the beliefs and understanding about God of the various writers of the Old Testament, though we shall only understand what each one writes, as we consider the whole pattern of their thought by considering all that they have written. We have tried to do this in Volume 2—see especially those sections of each chapter headed 'Message'.

We are now involved in the much more difficult task of discovering the Truth about God and His purposes which underlies the whole of the Old Testament. We shall try to answer such questions as (1) What is

THE WORD OF GOD

God like? (2) What was his purpose in creating men? (3) How shall
we serve Him? We shall draw on the insights of men from various
ages in order to reach our answers. We shall compare and contrast what
they have to say in order to get as full an understanding as we may.
We shall feel free to do so, believing that God Himself was at work in
the hearts and minds of people in every period of Israelite history, and
that each writer was led to some appreciation of the Truth. We shall
keep alert to the fact that it is possible to trace a growing and deepening
appreciation in the Old Testament which was the result of God's work
among His people through the centuries. We shall remember that,
even so, at the time of Christ there were some among God's people
who still failed to appreciate the corporate knowledge of God which
had been built up over the centuries. Such men rejected Christ when
he came. We shall only avoid their terrible mistake as we seek the help
of God in understanding all that we read.

## STUDY SUGGESTIONS

WORDS
1. Revelation is the giving and receiving of Truth. Which of the
following words has the same or a similar meaning to 'Truth' as it
is used in this chapter?
information   knowledge   relationship   theories   understanding
2. Each of the following words could be used to express part of the
meaning of the word 'revelation'. Which of the words would apply
to the activity of God, and which to the activity of men?
discover   learn   make known   recognize   teach   uncover
understand.

CONTENT
3. Why is there so little written in the Old Testament about the
Trinity?
4. What is the difference between the study of Old Testament Theology
and the study of Old Testament Religion?
5. What is the connection between the message of any one Old Testament book, e.g. Hosea, and the theology of the Old Testament?
6. Why is the help of God essential to our understanding of Old
Testament theology?

BIBLE
7. 'God's character does not change' (p. 12). Some of the Old
Testament writers call God 'the Rock' to express this idea. Study
Deuteronomy 32.1–43, and make a list of the things about the
character of God which are said not to change.

16

8. 'God works as a teacher' (p. 12).
   (a) Did the writers of the Old Testament think of God as a teacher? Use a Concordance to find illustrations for your answer.
   (b) What sort of things is God said to teach?

DISCUSSION

9. How would you answer an enquirer who asked: 'Why do we need to study the Old Testament? Surely it is sufficient for Christians to depend on the knowledge of God we find in the New Testament?'
10. In what ways, if any, are the things which God teaches us today different from those He taught His people in Old Testament times? Give examples from present-day life and from the Bible to support your answer.

# CHAPTER 1

# God

## THE UNITY OF GOD

Hear, O Israel: the LORD our God is one LORD. (Deuteronomy 6.4)

Jews give these words a central place in their worship, and allow them to influence all their thoughts about religious matters. They are the first words of the *Shema*, or Confession of Faith, which is used regularly in worship in the synagogues. They are also included among the verses of scripture contained in 'phylacteries' (Matt. 23.5). Phylacteries are small leather boxes which strict Jews wear, tied to their left upper arm, and to their forehead, in their daily private devotions (Deut. 6.8). If the Jews give these words a central place in their religion, then they must be important for our own understanding of the Old Testament. Jesus himself used these same words to explain to a scribe how he should serve God (Mark 12.29). So we should study them with care.

There are two important ideas contained in this brief statement:

1. First, God is named with the special title 'LORD'.
2. Secondly, God is said to be *one*.

Together, these ideas form a basis for our whole understanding of God revealed in the Old Testament.

### I. THE LORD

Whenever the word 'LORD' is printed in capital letters in the Old Testament, it stands as the translation of a special Hebrew title, which can best be written in Roman letters as YHWH. Most scholars agree that the best way to spell this title so that it can be spoken is 'YAHWEH', although nobody can say for certain what vowels were used when the name was first used among the Israelites. The earliest records give only the consonants, and by the time vowels were added the Jews believed that the name was too sacred to be spoken aloud, and always used a Hebrew word for 'master' instead, when they read their Scriptures. They added the vowels from this word to the special name, and this was the origin of *Jehovah*, which isn't a Hebrew word at all!

We have already studied in the earlier volumes of this course the origin and history of the name YHWH. It would be helpful to look again at the paragraphs that are relevant: See especially Volume 1, pp. 32–3, 48, 57, 60, 75.

For the Jews, YHWH stands as the name of the God who was known to Abraham, and to Moses, and who chose the Israelites to be His

18

special people. They knew that He had been active throughout their history, making Himself known to them through all their great leaders; and they believed that He had an important part for them to play in the history of the world. The name is interpreted in Exodus 3.14 as 'I am who I am', which suggests that God is what people discover Him to be through their worship and their history. He makes Himself known, and they are able to fill His name with meaning through their experience of Him.

## 2. ONE

The Hebrew word translated 'one' is the ordinary word used in counting, and does not of itself explain what the Jews meant when they said that 'the LORD our God is one LORD.' It could be interpreted in a number of different ways.

Some may have interpreted it: 'Yahweh is one, but there are others.'

More likely, some believed: 'Yahweh is the only God for Israel, but there are other gods for other peoples'. The other nations worship gods who share their power with lesser deities, but Yahweh's power is supreme in Israel.

Most certainly 'The LORD is One' came to mean that 'Yahweh, the God of Israel, is the only God; all others are mere idols with no real existence and no power.'

Probably the great leaders in Israel, throughout the period covered by the Old Testament, understood more fully than other people of their time that Yahweh is the only God. The mass of the people, like the peoples of neighbouring lands, went on speaking about other gods as though they had power and importance, and only gradually came to understand the fuller truth. And even the leaders may not have understood the full significance of what they believed about the LORD. Often they acted upon their faith without being able to say clearly what they believed. Let us look briefly at the way in which belief in the unity of God affected the lives of some of the outstanding characters of the Old Testament.

The Patriarchs were naturally influenced by the thoughts and beliefs of their own time. They expressed feelings of wonder, mystery, and even fear which were stirred in them by some powerful natural objects: fine trees, fast-flowing rivers, tall mountains, etc. (see p. 14). It is quite possible that their family had, before Abraham's time, given their main devotion to the moon-god, Sin. They had lived near Ur, and later near Haran, both places where this god was worshipped (Gen. 11.31).

But Abraham became aware of the presence and authority of the one God, and gave obedience and devotion to Him (Gen. 12.1–3). A later writer suggests that Abraham did not know the proper name of the LORD, and called Him 'El Shaddai' (Exod. 6.2, 3). But the important

19

'The great leaders in Israel understood more fully than other men that Yahweh is the only God. But most nations in Old Testament times believed in many gods' (p. 19).

This Babylonian boundary stone from the time of Nebuchadnezzar (605–562 BC) is carved with symbols of gods whose protection was asked for when the boundary was first marked out. Greater gods are represented by the suns and moon at the top, and lesser gods by the animals lower down.

fact is that, from the time of his call, Abraham served the one God, and felt no responsibility to serve other gods. More than this, he believed that what he did through service to the one God would affect all other peoples: 'by you all the families of the earth shall bless themselves' (Gen. 12.3). It is doubtful whether Abraham or his immediate descendants realized that because the one God had come to have a unique place in their lives, they must in the end recognize that other gods do not exist. They simply served the one God and ignored the gods that were worshipped by other peoples.

The Israelites who took part in the Exodus had much the same attitude. Moses came to them as a messenger from 'the LORD, the God of your fathers' (Exod. 3.15). They responded rather reluctantly to his call to leave Egypt, but there is no evidence that they feared the gods of the Egyptians. They celebrated the LORD's victory over the Egyptians, but did not describe it as a victory over the gods of Egypt (Exod. 15.21). The later victory song of Exodus 15.1–18 does mention other gods, but simply describes how powerless they were compared with the LORD, who 'will reign for ever and ever' (v. 18).

The Ten Commandments express the idea that the Israelites have a duty to worship and serve the LORD, and that they must not serve other gods (Exod. 20.2–3). Moses probably recognized the supremacy of the LORD so completely that for him other gods were nothing. But some of the Israelites did not fully understand these commandments. They knew they themselves should only serve the LORD, but they did not deny the power of other gods served by other nations.

Later, in the time of the Judges and the Kings of united Israel, many Israelites accepted the authority of the LORD in Israel, but also believed that other gods had their own areas of power and importance (Judg. 11.24; 1 Sam. 26.19, 20). Some of their stories suggest that the LORD was at conflict with other gods, and could defeat them (1 Sam. 5.1–5).

In other passages in the Old Testament, e.g. Deuteronomy 32.8, and Psalm 82.1–4, God is said to have given authority to lesser gods, 'sons of god', enabling them to rule the other nations, but leaving them responsible to the LORD for what they did. These passages show us part of the way in which the idea became accepted by the whole community, that God is fully in control of history, not only in Israel but in the whole creation.

The same idea is expressed in other Psalms (Pss. 96.4; 135.5). But the emphasis here is on the idea that the LORD is supreme, and there is nobody to challenge His authority (Pss. 86.8; 89.6; 95.3). The LORD is 'God of gods' (Ps. 136.2).

In conflict with these ideas, there was still a widespread belief among the Israelites that, although the LORD was their God who helped them in battle, they needed also to worship the fertility gods of Palestine, the Baalim, to ensure good crops and large families. This idea may have persisted especially among the descendants of other peoples who remained in Palestine after the twelve tribes settled there, and who eventually accepted the rule of David, and came to think of themselves as Israelites. Jezebel encouraged the worship of the fertility gods, because Baal had an important place in the religion of her own people, the Phoenicians. Elijah challenged this idea, and his own attitude is clear from these words spoken at Mount Carmel: 'How long will you go limping with two different opinions? If the LORD is God follow him, but if Baal, then follow him' (1 Kings 18.21). Yet the worship of the Baalim remained a source of conflict in Israel, right up to the time of the Exile. Jeremiah condemned the common practice of burning incense to the Baalim (Jer. 7.9; 11.13). To him this practice was as bad as murder or adultery: they were all abominations.

The unknown prophet of the Exile, the writer of Isaiah 40–55, was the first who expressed quite clearly the idea that the gods served by other nations simply do not exist, and that the LORD is God of all nations (Isa. 44.6; 45.22; 46.9; etc.). This prophet explained carefully what is involved in the belief that 'the LORD our God is one LORD'. He saw that, if this is true, then the LORD must be the Creator (Isa. 40.12, 22), and must have control of all past history (Isa. 40. 23, 24; 41.2–4); and all future destiny (Isa. 40.8–10; 42.8, 9; 43.13). The LORD is the one whom all men must serve (Isa. 45.8, 22–23). These ideas need careful study, and we shall return to them in the remaining sections of this chapter.

## STUDY SUGGESTIONS

WORDS

1. Write down as simply and directly as you can the meaning of the word 'God'. What difference does it make to your definition whether you believe in one God, or many gods?
2. 'The LORD our God is one LORD.' Which two of the following words have the same, or nearly the same meaning as the word *one* in this sentence?
   equal   identical   isolated   only   same   sole   united   whole

CONTENT

3. What is the connection between each of the following names for God, and the title YHWH?
   JEHOVAH   YAHWEH   The LORD
4. What difference was there between the attitude of the Israelites to gods of other nations, and their attitude to the Baalim.
5. Describe three ideas which the writer of Isaiah 40—55 derived from his belief that the LORD is the only God.

22

BIBLE

6. Use a Concordance to discover what the writers of the Psalms said about *idols*. In what way did they say that idols were different from the LORD?

7. Use a Concordance to discover what the various writers of the Old Testament had to say about the god *Chemosh*.
(a) Did any of them suppose that he had any power to affect the lives of the Moabites?
(b) Did they suppose that he could affect the lives of the Israelites? Give chapter and verse references to support your answers.

DISCUSSION

8. What attitude do you think the Patriarchs would have had towards the gods of Hinduism, if they had visited India? What should be the attitude of Christians to these gods?

9. (a) If we believe that there is only one God, does that prevent us from believing in other spiritual beings?
(b) What evidence can you discover in the Old Testament, that the Israelites believed in spirits directed and controlled by God, after the time of Deutero-Isaiah? (Look, for example, at Daniel and Zechariah, using a Concordance.)

10. 'The gods served by other nations simply do not exist' (p. 22). Do you think Deutero-Isaiah would have taken a different attitude to the religion of a people who believe in one supreme God, as for example that of the Batonga of Zambia, who believe in Leza.

# THE LORD AND CREATION

Have you not known? Have you not heard?
The LORD is the everlasting God,
the Creator of the ends of the earth.
(Isaiah 40.28)

The Babylonians believed that the world was created as a result of conflict between gods and goddesses: Marduk was victorious over Tiamat, and created the sky and earth from her body (see Vol. 1, p. 134).

The Persians believed that the world was the battle-field for a continuing conflict between Ormazd and Ahriman. They expected Ormazd, the god of goodness, to be victorious, but the battle was not yet over; the struggle between these gods continued (see Vol. 1, p. 150).

The Israelites took a totally different view of creation. Because the LORD is the only God, they believed that creation is entirely His doing.

'In the beginning God created the heavens and the earth. . . . And God saw everything that he had made, and behold it was very good' (Gen. 1.1 and 31). There is no opposing power of evil independent of God, active from eternity, and involved in creation (Isa. 41.4; 43.10; 44.6).

It is true that God's part in creation as the one God, neither hindered nor encouraged by others, is most fully expressed by writers in the later period of Old Testament thought. Deutero-Isaiah belonged to the time of the Exile, and Genesis 1 comes from the P-traditions which were incorporated in the Torah at the end of the Exile (see Vol. 2, p. 29). But similar and related ideas are found in earlier writings. The second account of creation (Gen. 2.4–25) comes from the J-traditions, which may have been compiled in the time of Solomon. Two of the Psalms which express praise to the LORD for his activity in creation, imply that it was all His doing (Pss. 8, 104). The exact date of the composition of these Psalms is not known, but Psalm 8 comes from a collection of Psalms which were perhaps gathered between 1000 and 900 BC (see Vol. 2, p. 100).

Several important ideas follow from the belief that 'God created the heavens and the earth':

## 1. THE LORD IS ALMIGHTY

Exodus 6.3 records that the Patriarchs called the LORD *El Shaddai*, and in the RSV this is translated 'God Almighty'. The name *Shaddai* was used at many different times during the history of Israel. If you recall the probable dates of the following writings you will realize that this name belongs to the periods of the kings, the exile, and the return, as well as the time of the Patriarchs: Isaiah 13.6; Ezekiel 1.24; Job 40.2; Joel 1.15. Scholars disagree about the exact meaning of this name, but in the Septuagint it is most often translated by a Greek word which means 'Ruler of all'. This implies that all things are under God's control. Nothing has power to defeat His purposes (Isa. 43.13; Job 9.4–12).

## 2. THE LORD CONTROLS NATURE

God exercises His power over the natural world in two separate but related ways.

(a) He has set the natural order of things in motion. By His authority day follows night, harvest follows seedtime (Gen. 8.22; Jer. 31.35, 36; 33.20). *Science* is the study of this natural order. Scientists today experiment in order to discover in detail just how the world works. They try to understand the forms of nature so as to be able to control and use them. They know far more than people did in Old Testament times, but they have the belief that there is order and regularity in

'All things are under God's control—He has set the natural order of things in motion. The Israelites believed that God continues to be active in and through His creation' (pp. 24, 26).

A Chinese farmer waters his crops each morning, confident that the orderly progress of the seasons will bring first the growth and then the harvest.

A wartime congregation in Scotland pray that God will take their side and give them victory over their enemies.

What is your opinion of these two attitudes to God's activity?

nature. The Israelites believed that the regular patterns of the natural world come from God's design and activity.

(b) But the Israelites also believed that God continues to be active in and through His creation (Amos 5.8; Ps. 145.15, 16), and that even the regular patterns of nature depend upon God for their continuity (Job 9.5–7; 12.15).

### 3. THE LORD WORKS MIRACLES THROUGH NATURE

The Israelites' belief that God is active in the normal sequences of nature gives us a clue to their attitude to miracles. Two ideas which are common today do not fit in with those we find in the Old Testament:

(a) The idea that God sometimes breaks into nature and history for sudden action conflicts with Old Testament thought, because it denies the reality of His *continuing* presence and activity.

(b) The idea that God has to overcome and redirect the forces of nature in order to achieve His purposes, falsely suggests that nature is in some sense separate from and even contrary to His will.

The Old Testament holds together the idea that creation is well-designed and properly ordered, with the idea that God is able to work in and through nature. In order to understand Old Testament ideas about the miracles described, we need to see them as illustrating how God uses the forces of nature, rather than as showing His conquest and disturbance of the normal course of events.

Sometimes the writers of the Old Testament emphasized strange and unusual happenings as evidence of God's activity, but more often they described God as using ordinary natural events to achieve His purposes. The plagues in Egypt probably were all normal events in the climate and conditions of that country, but their timing and their severity were seen as evidence of God at work. The drought in Elijah's time, and the lightning which burnt up his offering, were natural events, but none the less they were under the LORD's control.

### 4. THE LORD IS GOD OF WISDOM

Since God has created all things, and all things are under His control, He possesses complete knowledge of creation (Ps. 147.4, 5). This idea is expressed in Job 38 through a contrast between Job's ignorance and the LORD's knowledge. Job 28.20–27 describes God's knowledge, and the wisdom that comes from it. See also Job 12.13. Many biblical writers tell of men having understanding because the LORD has given it to them (e.g. Exod. 31.3; Ps. 119.66; Isa. 11.2).

### 5. THE LORD HAS A PURPOSE FOR HIS CREATION

The two stories of creation in Genesis both give a central place to the making of human beings. In Genesis 1 men and women are the climax of creation. In Genesis 2 God prepares a garden for man, and then creates a mate for him. God gives mankind responsibility to use the world wisely and with good purpose (Gen. 1.28, compare 2.15). Throughout the history of Israel we read of people who were called by God to help fulfil His purposes. Israel itself had a special place in God's plans as the means of bringing His blessing to all mankind. We shall study the nature of God's purposes more fully in the later sections of this book, but it is important to recognize that mankind has a central place in God's plans.

## 6. EVIL CANNOT STOP THE LORD'S WORK

We have already seen that Old Testament writers rejected the idea that there is a power of evil which has existed alongside the LORD from eternity. They recognized that there is evil in the world, but saw it as a result of corruption: People can choose good, but they often choose evil instead. The story of the Fall in Genesis 3 expresses this idea, and it is repeated in such verses as Genesis 6.12; Exodus 32.7, etc. We shall need to study in a later chapter the question raised in the Old Testament of the existence of other corruptible beings (ch. 2). Here it is sufficient to notice that the powers of evil are always described as being less than God. God's power is supreme, and His purposes will be fulfilled.

## STUDY SUGGESTIONS

WORDS

1. Which of the following verbs is nearest in meaning to the verb *to create*?
   to construct    to erect    to establish    to manufacture    to produce
2. Which of the following words best describes the nature of Old Testament Theology? (If necessary, first use a dictionary to make sure you know their meaning.)
   dualism    monotheism    polytheism

CONTENT

3. (a) How would you describe the work of scientists?
   (b) In what chief ways do the Old Testament writers think differently about nature from the ways in which scientists describe it?
4. A dictionary defines a miracle as 'an act or event which does not follow the laws of nature; remarkable and surprising event'.
   (a) What is your opinion of this definition?
   (b) What difference does it make to our attitude to miracles, that the 'laws of nature' are becoming better known through the work of scientists?

BIBLE

5. Use a Concordance to discover which books of the Old Testament contain the verb *to create*, and the nouns *creator* and *creature*.
   (a) To which periods of Israelite history do these books belong?
   (b) Which of the prophets was probably the earliest to use this term?
6. (a) Examine the use of the words *work* and *works* in the Psalms, and make a list of things that are described as the LORD's work.
   (b) are the things you have listed for (a) above mainly activities in nature, or are they mainly activities in the hearts of men? Give some examples of each.

DISCUSSION

7. God is almighty.
   (a) Is there anything that He will not do? If so, what?
   (b) Is there anything He cannot do? If so, what?
8. (a) What do you think was God's main purpose in creation?
   (b) How far is this purpose fulfilled among mankind today?


## THE LORD AND HISTORY

Thus says the LORD ...
Who is like me? Let him proclaim it,
Let him declare and set it forth before me.
Who has announced from of old the things to come?
Let them tell us what is yet to be.
Fear not, nor be afraid;
have I not told you from of old and declared it?
And you are my witnesses!
Is there a God besides me!
There is no Rock; I know not any.

(Isaiah 44.6–8)

The Israelites were the first of all the peoples of the ancient Near East to write connected accounts of history. Other nations built monuments to celebrate their great victories, but they had nothing to say about their defeats. They were unable to see any organized pattern of events which could encourage them to write history books.

The reason for this is easy to see. Most nations believed in many gods, and that each god showed his power when his own people were victorious. But when they were defeated, they believed that this was because their god had been defeated too. For them, any connected account of history would need to explain the rise and fall of the gods that they served. Myths about the relationships between the gods were composed, especially among the Greeks. Human history was regarded as the accidental result of conflicts between the gods.

Those who accepted dualism shared much the same view of history. They saw the whole of history as the outcome of conflict between the forces of good and the forces of evil. Men were involved in the conflict, but they could only guess at the underlying cause of events. The real battle, they believed, was between the gods.

The Israelites, on the other hand, believed in 'one LORD', and they saw history as the result of relationships between the LORD and men. This was part of human experience, and could be interpreted and understood by those who looked for the ways of the LORD in all that happened. The J-traditions provided the basis for the first connected account of history among the Israelites. The editors of this tradition related the whole of history to the LORD's call of Abraham. God had promised that certain things would happen as a reward for Abraham's obedience (Gen. 12.1–3), and in the course of time He fulfilled these promises. All the later historical records in the Old Testament were based upon this same belief: that history is the result of the LORD's initiative, and men's response.

## I. THE LORD'S INITIATIVE

All the major events of Israelite history are described as being the result of the LORD's initiative. It was the LORD who took the first step, and His people followed. We have already noticed the LORD's call of Abraham. It was the LORD who brought Joseph and his brothers into Egypt (Gen. 45.6–8). The LORD rescued His people from Egypt (Exod. 3.7, 8). The LORD enabled Joshua to lead the people into the Promised Land (Josh. 1.1–9). The LORD raised up judges to rescue His people from their enemies (Judg. 2.18). Samuel doubted the wisdom of appointing kings in Israel, but in the end the LORD chose Saul to be king (1 Sam. 9.15, 16). The LORD raised up prophets to guide the kings and the people (2 Sam. 7.4, 5, etc.). The LORD even raised up foreign nations to punish His people for their disobedience (Amos 6.14), and a foreign ruler, Cyrus, to set them free from their exile (Isa. 44.28).

All through the Old Testament we find the writers describing the LORD at work. They were chiefly interested in His activities among His own people, the Israelites. But many of the prophets spoke also of God's judgement on other nations (e.g. Amos 1.3—2.3; Isa. 13–23; Jer. 46—51; Ezek. 25—32, etc.). From Genesis 12.3 onward, the future of all nations is seen to be tied up with the LORD's activities in Israel. Jerusalem has an important place in the visions of the future presented by many of the prophets (Isa. 2.1–4; Jer. 3.17; Joel 3.1; Zech. 2.11, 12, etc.).

## 2. MAN'S RESPONSE

God's initiative in history is always through His relationship with men. Abraham, Moses, David, Isaiah, etc. all influenced the course of history because they responded to the LORD's call. They were outstanding men because they obeyed the LORD, and He was able to use them for His purposes.

But the writers of the Old Testament were realists; they recognized that such people were rare, and that for every one devoted leader there were multitudes of disobedient people, both among the Israelites and from other nations. How could the LORD influence history when so few were responsive to His will? The Old Testament writers gave several different answers to this question. We can summarize them under four headings:

1. *The influence of one obedient man is more far-reaching than that of many disobedient people.* For example, Joseph was badly treated by his brothers and by Potiphar's wife, but because he remained faithful to the LORD, he lived to save the Egyptians from the worst effects of a severe famine, and also provided a new home for his relatives. 'There is none so discreet and wise as you are' (Gen. 41.39).

Many of those who were obedient to the LORD were not popular in their own life-time, and were only later recognized as men who had known the ways of the LORD. Isaiah of Jerusalem was disappointed that the people of his time would not listen to him, but he believed that later they would see that he had been right, and would be influenced by his teaching and example (Isa. 30.8–11). Similarly Jeremiah was despised by the people of Judah, but after the destruction of Jerusalem those who wrote Lamentations were able to recognize that events were a fulfilment of what he had said (see Vol. 2, p. 120). The written records of the words and actions of such men have continued to influence the Jews right down through their history until today.

2. *Even those who do not know the LORD may serve His purposes.* The Assyrians did not suppose they were serving the LORD when they attacked Jerusalem. Their Rabshakeh urged the people not to listen if the king of Judah should say 'The LORD will deliver us'. No god among all the nations, had been able to save any of the peoples from the Assyrians (Isa. 36.18–20, and compare Isa. 10.5–11). Yet Isaiah believed that the LORD was using the Assyrians to punish Judah (Isa. 7.18–20). Similarly, at the end of the exile the LORD raised up Cyrus to set His people free, even though Cyrus himself did not know that he was serving the LORD (Isa. 45.4, 5).

But the writers also came to realize that such people may either (a) come to know that they are serving the LORD, as Deutero-Isaiah hoped in the case of Cyrus (Isa. 45.3); or (b) go on to do things contrary to the will of the LORD, and so come under judgement, as in the case of the Assyrians (Isa. 10.12–19).

3. *Even those who disobey the LORD are in their own way responding to Him.* According to the Old Testament writers, no man's action is fully understood unless it is seen as the result of his relationship to the LORD: either accepting or rejecting His will. Pharaoh's refusal to let the Israelites leave Egypt is described in this way: 'the LORD said . . . I will harden his heart so that he will not let the people go' (Exod. 4.21). This implies that the LORD had given Pharaoh a fair opportunity to do His will. When Pharaoh refused to respond, he came under God's judgement, and was punished. The same idea is found in the account of Isaiah's call. God had chosen Isaiah to be His messenger to Judah. The people of Judah were given their opportunity to respond to the LORD, but they rejected Isaiah's message and so came under His judgement (Isa. 6.9, 10).

4. *The LORD will bring an end to evil, and will establish righteousness on His Day.* The Israelites believed that history was leading somewhere, that all the LORD's activities among men would eventually bring a time when all men would serve the LORD (Isa. 65.17). There would then be peace and justice on earth (Isa. 65.21; Micah. 4.4). Those who rejected the way of the LORD would not for ever be able to disturb the life of society, and bring suffering and injustice. They would face judgement (Zeph. 1.15), while the righteous would share the new order under God's rule (Joel 2.32).

## STUDY SUGGESTIONS

WORDS

1. 'The LORD's *initiative*'. Which one of the following words best expresses the same idea as *initiative*.
   loving    originating    planning    prompting    teaching
2. 'Abraham, Moses, David, Isaiah, etc. all influenced the course of history' (p. 30).
   Which *two* of the following words best express the same ideas as the word 'course' in this sentence?
   direction    duration    orderliness    outcome    syllabus

CONTENT

3. What prompted the Israelites to write a connected account of the development of history?
4. Were the Israelites interested in the history of other nations?
   If so, in what way was that interest expressed by the writer of the Old Testament?

BIBLE

5. The initiative of the LORD in the Old Testament is often expressed

by the use of the phrase 'to raise up'. Use a Concordance to examine the use of this phrase in different parts of the Old Testament.
(a) How many named people are said to have been 'raised up' by the LORD? Write out as full a list as you can.
(b) What positions in Israel were held by men 'raised up' by the LORD? Were they Prophets? or priests? Give references to support your answer.
6. Choose one of the ideas listed in the section 'Man's Response' (pp. 30, 31), and provide further illustrations of the ideas from your knowledge of Old Testament History.

DISCUSSION
7. 'It is foolish to expect theology to provide a key to the interpretation of history. Human history is the story of changing human relation-ships, and only as it is accepted as this can it be rightly understood.' Do you agree with this statement? Give reasons for your answer.
8. 'The world is a better place today than it was a century ago.' Do you agree? Give reasons for your answer.
9. 'Each race, nation, or tribe will find greater benefit in studying the history of its own people, than in studying the history of other people's.'
(a) Do you agree? How does your answer affect the interest you take in the history of Israel?
(b) In what way, if any, are the historical records of the Old Testament different from the historical records of other nations?

## THE LORD AND MORALITY

Listen to me, my people,
and give ear to me, my nation;
for a law will go forth from me,
and my justice for a light to the peoples.
(Isaiah 51.4)

Every human society develops its own pattern of accepted forms of behaviour, in order to restrict causes of conflict and to enable people to live together in peace. Such a pattern of accepted behaviour is called 'morality', or a code of ethics. By regular use it becomes part of the customs of the people who use it, though many other sorts of activity may also be called customs.

Usually systems of morality are built up over long periods of time, and many different things affect the particular form accepted by a tribe or people, e.g.:

(a) A great leader from the past may have set an example which his people admired, and therefore continued to copy;

(b) The extent to which people depend on each other for the necessities of life affects the relationships between them. Their need for food, shelter, protection from enemies, etc., affects people's customary behaviour as a group, and the pattern of their morality;

(c) The group's experience of life together shows them that certain ways of behaving have creative results in their relationships, and other ways are found to be destructive. These experiences affect what the group as a whole accepts as moral behaviour;

(d) Relationships with more powerful tribes and nations will lead a group to act in ways which will bring harmony and avoid conflict.

In ways like these a morality develops which controls the behaviour of the group, and its members will disapprove and even punish any individual who acts against the best interests of the group.

Our interest here is to consider whether a people's religious understanding and experiences affect the development of their pattern of morality. This depends on how far people believe that their religion concerns human relationships, as well as relationships with the divine. The answer varies, in fact, with the sort of religion that is followed. Let us consider the probable influence of polytheism, dualism, and monotheism.

## 1. POLYTHEISM

The worshipper's main concern is to persuade the god to treat him with favour. Usually he does this by offering sacrifices and performing rituals, and sometimes by behaving in particular ways towards other people. However, each different god requires different responses, so a man who worships more than one god is likely to be faced with conflicting loyalties. He may behave in one way to please a particular god, but his religion may teach that another god will be displeased by this behaviour. No single pattern of behaviour will enable him to please all his gods at once. His religion cannot give him a sure guide for his behaviour, but will drive him to act first in one way, and then in another. Thus we see that polytheism is the form of religion least likely to have a deep influence on the development of an accepted pattern of morality. It is the most likely to give people the feeling that they can never really know the difference between right and wrong. Instead, they will be taught to do what other people expect them to do.

## 2. DUALISM

In its simplest form, dualism is the belief that there are two gods who are in conflict with each other, both fighting for supreme power. Usually in such religions one of the gods is believed to be the god of goodness, and the other the god of evil. And according to this belief, human beings have a choice; they can serve one god or the other, but they cannot remain neutral. But the standard of judgement cannot be based on the will of either of the gods, because each could claim that his way was best. In fact the judgement—i.e. the choice of following one god or the other—is based on the patterns of behaviour that have become accepted by the people. The god which supports these is regarded as good, the god which does not, as evil. Dualism has no power of its own to create, or even to help to create, a new pattern of morality. (See Vol. 1, *Religion of the Persians*, pp. 150–2.)

### 3. MONOTHEISM

Monotheism begins with belief in one God who is creator and sustainer of all life and being. People recognize such a god as being both active and purposeful. A man can respond to God, either by accepting and living by God's purposes as he becomes aware of them, or else by rejecting them and disobeying God. In such a religion, good is seen to be everything that is in tune with the purposes of God, and evil to be everything that is contrary. The People of Israel developed a pattern of morality which they believed to be in tune with the purposes of God. The more closely they came to understand God, the nearer they came to developing an ideal morality. The more they were aware of God's purposes, the more clearly they recognized their responsibility to serve Him, and the possibility of judgement if they did not.

The Ten Commandments provided the basis for all later development of Israelite morality. They were the essential guidelines for a way of life which was entirely acceptable to the LORD. 'You shall therefore keep my statutes and my ordinances, by doing which a man shall live. I am the LORD' (Lev. 18.5).

In their later codes of law, the Israelites attempted to interpret the basic guidelines in the light of the circumstances of a particular time. What was right for nomads was not necessarily appropriate for a settled agricultural people. What was right for a member of a tribe of Israel in the time of the Judges was not necessarily appropriate for people living under the rule of David. What was right for life in Palestine was not necessarily appropriate for life in exile in Babylon. But always the guide to what was right was the will of the LORD. What He wanted from His people, they accepted as the way of righteousness. The Ten Commandments remained as a basic pattern for obedience which would not change, though it was expressed in different ways at different times.

The prophets were continually challenging Israelites to live according to the patterns of morality which they had received from the LORD. Often the prophets had to deal with situations which arose because many of the Israelites did not understand the special importance of morality in their religion. Continually they were tempted to follow the pattern of other religions, and to suppose that what the LORD chiefly required from his people was worship and sacrifice. They found it difficult to understand that even though they took part in the sacrifices and feast days, the LORD was not necessarily satisfied with their service. The prophets had to repeat again and again that obedience is better than sacrifice (1 Sam. 15.22; Isa. 1.12–17; Prov. 21.3, etc.). They did not deny the importance of worship, but made it quite clear that worship and morality belong together in the service of the LORD.

## STUDY SUGGESTIONS

WORDS

1. Which of the following definitions most fully describes the Old Testament idea of morality at its best?

(a) A way of life that will win the approval of the group to which a man belongs.

(b) A way of life that is appropriate to the purpose of life both for the individual and his group.

(c) A way of life that will bring material prosperity to the individual and his group.

2. 'They were the essential guidelines for a way of life which was entirely acceptable to the LORD' (p. 34).

Which one of the following words best expresses the meaning of 'guidelines' in that sentence?

designs      directions      plans      schemes      suggestions

CONTENT

3. Old Testament morality had a quite different basis from the morality of Egypt or Babylon. What was the difference?

4. Although the patterns of morality described in the Bible changed from age to age, they were all in accordance with the will of the LORD. Do you agree with this statement? Give reasons for your opinion, with examples to support it.

BIBLE

5. (a) Study Psalm 119 and list all the different words used to mean rules which describe the will of the LORD. Then,

(b) Use a dictionary to discover the precise meaning of each of these words.

6. (a) Use a Concordance to discover which of the words that you have listed from Psalm 119 were also used by the prophet Jeremiah.

(b) Do many of the other prophets make much use of these words? If not, in what other ways did they challenge 'the Israelites to live according to the patterns of morality which they had received from the LORD'? (p. 34). Isa. 24.5, and Jer. 11.3 may help you to answer.

DISCUSSION

7. Discover what you can about a modern form of polytheism (e.g. Hinduism), and consider whether it has produced any distinct pattern of morality.
8. Some forms of religion have required customs which are widely believed to be immoral (e.g. human sacrifice). Patterns of morality accepted in the Old Testament as coming from the LORD are widely recognized as good, even by those who do not acknowledge the authority of the LORD. Should a religion be judged by the quality of life that it encourages? Give your reasons.

## THE TRINITY IN THE OLD TESTAMENT

We have seen that the most distinctive idea of the Jewish faith is the Unity of God: 'Hear, O Israel: the LORD our God is one LORD.' This idea was very different from the ideas held by people of other nations of the ancient Near East. At first, it was one that seemed strange to the Israelites themselves, and was not quickly grasped and understood. But gradually, through the centuries, as the LORD worked among His people in the varying situations of their history, more and more of them came to appreciate the importance of this belief in the Unity of God.

We have seen that the idea affected their understanding of such important matters as creation, history, and morality. It transformed their whole understanding of human life, and presented them with new responsibilities as they tried to live out their lives in the light of this faith.

In the New Testament we see the beginning of a new idea about God—the idea which was eventually formulated as the doctrine of the Trinity; Father, Son, and Holy Spirit. New Testament writers described the Son as being in existence, and at work, from the beginning of creation (Col. 1.16); He who came to live a human life, was God from the beginning (Phil. 2.6). Similarly, they described the Holy Spirit as 'eternal' (Heb. 9.14). The same Spirit of God that enabled them to preach the Gospel had been given to Abraham through faith (Gal. 3.14), and had inspired the prophets of the Old Testament (1 Peter 1.10–12; 1 Cor. 2.11).

Some readers may ask why the idea of the Trinity was not clearly revealed in the Old Testament times. The answer seems to be that it was more important for the Jews to grasp the significance of God's Unity. No human being can fully understand what God is. It would

have been easy for the Jews to misunderstand the truth about His
triune nature. They might have tried to worship three separate gods,
and even this limited form of polytheism would have prevented them
from reaching the truth about creation, history, and morality. For this
truth could not be fully understood without an appreciation of the
Unity of God.

It is equally important for Christians today to recognize the Unity
of God, and to be aware of the difference this makes to our understanding of creation, history, and morality. However great the importance
of our belief in Father, Son, and Holy Spirit, we must not lose sight of
the fact that the three Persons are one God-head. Whatever is true
about the Unity of God, is also true of the Trinity, and response to
God's single purpose for us in creation and history is the true basis for
Christian morality.

But belief in the Trinity is not simply a useful theory, or a carefully
devised scheme of thought which satisfies our desire for an understanding of God. It is the only way we have, in human thought and
language, of expressing a mystery. According to the New Testament,
the God who revealed himself to the Israelites in Old Testament times
*was* Father, Son, and Holy Spirit, even though they were only aware of
Him as the one LORD, and had no appreciation of his Triune (Three-in-
One) nature.

Is there then any evidence that men of Old Testament times began
to think in ways which would gradually lead to the New Testament
doctrine of the Trinity? Were they, without knowing it, sharing in
experiences which pointed to the Triune God? In their struggle to put
into words what they experienced of God, were they using terms that
would later be used in expressing the doctrine of the Trinity?

Having put the question in this particular way, we find that a number
of Old Testament ideas were eventually taken up and used by New
Testament writers in order to express what they needed to say about the
Trinity. These ideas related to God's activity within creation, and in
relationship with mankind, and they were expressed in such terms as
*Wisdom* and *the Spirit of the LORD*.

As we shall see in the following paragraphs, each of these terms
was at one time used as a way of talking about the LORD. But later
writers used them to describe separate impersonal forces under the
LORD's control. Then, in poetic literature, they were used to describe
independent beings believed to be active in their own way, though
responsive to the LORD. It seems certain that when the Jews used these
words they were not intending to describe separate personalities
within the God-head, but it is equally certain that the New Testament
writers did use the same ideas to describe the three Persons of the
Trinity.

Many people believe that in this way the LORD prepared the Jew. for the fuller revelation which was to come through Jesus Christ, and that a real foundation for New Testament thought was prepared. Let us look now in more detail at the ideas of *Wisdom* and *the Spirit of the LORD*.

## 1. WISDOM

In the biblical writings produced before the exile, Wisdom is simply a quality. God's own activities show this Wisdom (Jer. 10.12). Men possess Wisdom as a gift from the LORD (Deut. 4.6; 1 Kings 3.28; 4.29). In Job, Wisdom is described as something that God knows and understands (Job 28.23, 24). He alone can 'search it out' (verse 27), He alone fully possesses it. But men will find it by obedience to the LORD (verse 28).

In Proverbs 1—8, Wisdom is described as a woman. She is active and alive, and does what she thinks right. She offers understanding to all who will listen to her. In most of these chapters we may regard this way of describing wisdom as simply picture language—a device of poetry, a way of expressing a difficult idea in words which people would quickly understand. But in Proverbs 8.22–36 we find new ideas of wisdom, described in a different way, e.g. Wisdom was created by the LORD at the beginning of His work (Prov. 8.22). Wisdom was 'like a master workman' (8.30); Wisdom found delight in all that the LORD made (8.30, 31); Wisdom provides life to all who find her (8.35). We may think that these expressions too, are poetic forms, but they provided a starting place for ideas which were developed further in the books which now form the Apocrypha.

There, in the book called the Wisdom of Solomon (7.22—8.1), Wisdom is described in words which are closely related to terms used in the New Testament to describe Jesus, the Son of God (Col. 1.15–17; Heb. 1.2, 3). What started out as a poetical description of the Wisdom of God, became an expression of something far more significant than the writers of the Old Testament or the Apocrypha imagined. The way was prepared for discussion of the Person of Christ.

## 2. THE SPIRIT OF THE LORD

The word 'spirit' is used very often in the Old Testament. The translators who produced the RSV used a capital S to distinguish references to the Spirit of the LORD from those relating to other lesser spirits, and to the spirit of man. Yet the same Hebrew word is found in almost all places where the English word 'spirit' is used as the translation, whichever meaning is intended. The same Hebrew word is also translated in many places as *wind*, or *breath*.

Because the same Hebrew word is used in so many ways, it is not always easy to be certain which sense the writer intended in any particular verse. However, the translators have done their best in each case to discover the meaning intended, by examining the whole sentence and also the paragraph in which it stands, and thus to provide an accurate translation. Our interest here is in the Spirit of the LORD; we shall discuss other meanings in chapters 2 and 3.

In many passages the word 'Spirit' is used merely as another way of naming the LORD. But from very early times the word Spirit was used to describe an impersonal power under the control of the LORD, and used by Him to equip men for his service. This power enabled Moses to be a leader among the Israelites, and was given to others so that they might share his responsibilities (Num. 11.17, 25). In a similar way Elisha received power to follow as leader after Elijah was taken up (2 Kings 2.9, 10). This same power came on other people to equip them for their work; e.g. Gideon (Judg. 6.34), Samson (Judg. 14.6), Saul (1 Sam. 10.6, 10). In all these instances the Spirit produced dramatic effects in the lives of the people concerned, but there is nothing to suggest a personal relationship between the Spirit and the person receiving it.

At a later stage in the history of Israel the Spirit was thought to enable prophets to speak in the name of the LORD. The earliest prophets were not quick to accept this as an explanation of their authority, because they did not wish to be compared with the ecstatic spokesmen of the Baalim and other false gods, who claimed to be working as a result of inspiration received from the spirits of their gods. But Micah used the idea (Mic. 3.8); Ezekiel did also (Ezek. 8.3; 11.1, etc.); and others followed (Isa. 61.1; Zech 7.12; Joel 2.28).

Towards the end of the Old Testament period the writers increasingly used language which suggests that the Spirit of the LORD is a person, alive and active. The Spirit is said to do many things which in other passages are described as the work of the LORD. He abides with His people (Hag. 2.5); He leads (Ps. 143.10); He instructs (Neh. 9.20); He enables His people to live good lives (Ps. 51.10–12); He grieves over the sins of those who rebel against the LORD (Is. 63.10). The Spirit is everywhere present, so that nobody can escape from Him (Ps. 139.7).

The Jews never supposed that the Spirit was anything other than part of the essential nature of the LORD, just as the spirit of a man is an essential part of his human nature. But at the very beginning of the early Church Peter was able to quote Joel 2.28–32 in order to describe the work of the Holy Spirit (Acts 2.16–21). Again, the way had been prepared for new truths to be expressed in terms which were already familiar. The Jewish crowds were able to appreciate what Peter was saying on the first Pentecost, even though the theology of the Trinity was not fully developed. The Apostles were dealing with the same experiences of God which people in Old Testament times had known, and were learning to express them with the fuller understanding that was available through Christ. Later writers, including Paul, expressed the revelation of the Holy Spirit even more fully.

## STUDY SUGGESTIONS

WORDS

1. The Christian teaching about the Trinity is often expressed by saying that we believe in 'Three Persons; One God'. Which of the following terms are nearest in meaning to the word 'Persons' in that statement?
creatures     distinct beings     existences     separate individuals
realities.
2. The word 'unity' can be used in different ways. Whîch of the following definitions most fully expresses the meaning of the word in the phrase 'Unity of God'.
   (a) Every part working in harmony.
   (b) Sharing a common purpose, and working together to achieve it.
   (c) All one without distinctions.

CONTENT

3. 'Theology is the attempt to describe spiritual realities.'
   (a) Does this statement fully describe what you yourself understand by the word 'theology'?
   (b) How does this statement help us to appreciate the place of the Trinity in the Old Testament?
4. In what way does Joel 2.28–32 provide a link between Old Testament theology and New Testament theology?

BIBLE

5. Use a Concordance to discover how the phrase 'Word of God' (and also 'my word', 'thy word') is used in the Old Testament.
   What evidence can you find that the writers gradually developed an understanding of this phrase which prepared the way for its use in John 1?
6. Study the verses in the Old Testament where the idea of the 'breath' of God is used. Two Hebrew words are sometimes translated by the word 'breath'. What powers are possessed by the breath of God, according to these passages?

DISCUSSION

7. Some Christians suppose that Father, Son, and Holy Spirit are all one person, seen in different situations.

(a) Can you suggest reasons why that view of the Trinity is not accepted by the Church in general.

(b) What evidence is there in the Bible of the relationships between the three persons?

8. 'As yet the Spirit had not been given, because Jesus was not yet glorified' (John 7.39). How would you explain the meaning of this verse in the light of what has been said in this chapter?

# CHAPTER 2

# Other Spiritual Beings

## SPIRITS

In many parts of the world people have believed in a Supreme God, but have given their worship and service to lesser spirits. The Supreme God has seemed so remote and inaccessible that people have felt that there was little possibility of approaching him. These peoples have believed that many lesser spirits have had power to affect their lives directly. For this reason they have made sacrifices, and given offerings to these beings, hoping to gain their protection from trouble or sickness. In general, two sorts of spirits have been approached in worship;

(a) spirits of nature, believed to have power over the natural world and particularly over fertility,

(b) spirits of the dead, believed to have influence over the life of the community and of individuals.

We need to know the attitude of the writers of the Bible to the worship of spirits, because this will help us to form our own understanding of these matters, and enable us to respond in the right way to the revelation of God presented in the Bible. The Old Testament provides most of the help we need on this subject.

The first thing we discover as we examine the books of the Old Testament is that the Israelites did not think of the LORD as remote or inaccessible. He is always described as present among His people, actively making Himself known and desiring personal fellowship with them. All the Old Testament writings were produced by men who believed that they had had an experience of the living God, either as individuals, or through the life of the community. Again and again the prophets and poets urged the people to respond to the LORD in worship and service, and to find His blessing as a result. Nothing is clearer in the writings of the Old Testament than the reality of the presence and activity of the LORD.

For this reason, belief in other spiritual beings had a much less important place in the lives of the Israelites. The writers of the Old Testament never encouraged the worship of these lesser beings, and many of them openly condemned it as foolish and unworthy of those who know the LORD.

The nearest thing to worship of nature spirits described in the Old Testament is worship of the Baalim. We have seen that, in the time of the divided kingdoms, some of the Israelites supposed that they should

'Many peoples have believed that lesser spirits have power to affect men's lives, and have given them offerings, hoping to gain protection from trouble and sickness' (p. 42).

In Korea a Buddhist monk offers sacrifice to the protective deities at an open-air shrine. In Ghana a well-known medicine-man prepares to sacrifice a goat in order to 'kill' a patient's disease. In Luxembourg Christian clergy walk in procession carrying a 'miraculous' statue of the Virgin Mary, believed to bring health and prosperity.

What are your own beliefs about 'spirits' of nature, of ancestors, of saints, etc., and their power to affect people's lives?

worship the Baalim as well as the LORD. They thought the Baalim could ensure good crops for them, and large families. Elijah opposed this cult, because he saw that it was in danger of turning the Israelites from the service of the LORD (1 Kings 18.21). King Josiah's reform of religion included the destruction of things used in worship of the Baalim (2 Kings 23.4). Hosea and Jeremiah both condemned this worship (Hos. 9.10–17; Jer. 11.13). The LORD has created the universe and everything in it. These prophets knew that there are many forces in nature which human beings can learn to control as they discover more about them. Winds and water, fire and frost can destroy, or they can be used. But these powers are not 'spirits', to be worshipped instead of, or alongside, God. They have no power to think or feel, or to answer men's prayers.

Like many other peoples, some of the Israelites believed in ancestral spirits, and in their power to affect the lives of men. King Saul sought guidance from the spirit of the dead Samuel (1 Sam. 28.3–25). But Saul was going against his own better judgement, for we read that he had forbidden his people to seek help from the dead (1 Sam. 28.3, 9). The woman who was the medium in this story thought she was in contact with 'a god' (28.13). This is an important part of the danger involved in trying to make contact with the dead: the danger of giving them worship that really belongs to the LORD. The prophet Isaiah condemned such activities in Israel: 'Should not a people consult their God?' (Isa. 8.19). The Law Code of Deuteronomy includes mediums (i.e. people who try to contact the dead) among the things which are an abomination to the LORD (Deut. 18.11, 12). The Holiness Code warns that mediums defile those who turn to them (Lev. 19.31; 20.6), and that they must be punished (Lev. 20.27). We shall need to study the ideas of Old Testament writers about the dead in a later chapter, but what is important here is that the spirits of the dead were not to be worshipped. The Israelites honoured the memories of their ancestors, but were taught not to seek help from them. The reason was that help comes from the LORD (Ps. 121.1, 2).

In general, then, the Old Testament writers rejected the worship of spirits, and stressed that the LORD alone should be served.

## ANGELS

Although the Old Testament writers agree that there are no spirits, either of nature or of the dead, that should be worshipped, they do not deny the existence of other spiritual beings besides the LORD, who live to serve Him. In fact, throughout the Old Testament we find references to such beings. Often they are called Angels, but are given other titles too. We must now study what is said of these beings, keeping in mind that they are not independent of the LORD, but were created to serve him (Neh. 9.6).

The Hebrew word translated as 'angel' was probably first used to describe somebody who is 'sent' to do something, i.e. a messenger. The same word is used for human messengers in many parts of the Old Testament (e.g. Gen. 32.3, Isa. 18.2, Neh. 6.3). Sometimes we find it difficult to decide whether a writer is speaking or an angel or a man (e.g. 1 Kings 19.5, 7).

In the earliest writings of the Old Testament *the Angel of the LORD* is often mentioned. This use of the word 'angel' has a special interpretation which we examine separately later in this chapter (see p. 48). Groups of angels are mentioned quite early in the Old Testament, e.g. Jacob in his dream of a ladder between heaven and earth, saw the angels of God going up and down it (Gen. 28.12).

Later in the story of Jacob he met a company of angels, and said 'This is God's army' (Gen. 32.1, compare Josh. 5.14, 15). A similar idea is contained in the word 'hosts'. The expressions 'the hosts of heaven' (1 Kings 22.19) and 'the hosts of the heights' (Isa. 24.21) often refer to angels, although sometimes these phrases are used to speak of the stars. Notice also the 'council' of the holy ones (Ps. 89.7).

Sometimes the Old Testament writers seem to mean angels when they refer to 'gods' in a general way. Probably in the earlier periods some writers supposed that there were distinct and alien gods, but more often the writers emphasized the supremacy of the LORD, and declared that these spiritual beings served him (Pss. 82.1; 138.1). Psalm 97.7 is especially interesting, because the Psalmist denies that idols have any power, but accepts that there are spiritual beings which 'bow down before him'. Similarly the 'sons of God', sometimes translated 'heavenly beings' (see RSV footnotes), often seem to be obedient to the LORD, and should therefore be regarded as angels (Pss. 29.1; 89.6; Job 1.6); and so should the 'holy ones' (Deut. 33.2; Ps. 89.5; Zech. 14.5).

A number of special terms are used which seem to suggest that the Israelites believed in different sorts of angels, perhaps serving different purposes, e.g. the *Seraphim*, or fiery ones, who sing the praises of the LORD at his throne (Isa. 6.2, 6); and the *Cherubim* who are pictured as supporting the throne of the LORD (Ps. 18.10; Ezek. 10.15–17). Statues representing these beings were set up in the Temple, to remind those who worshipped of the heavenly hosts who also worshipped. The 'watchers' in Daniel 4.13, 17, 23 who announce the judgement of the LORD seem to be another sort of angel. Two angels are mentioned by name: Michael (Dan. 10.13, 21; 12.1) and Gabriel (Dan. 8.16; 9.21), The former is described as 'one of the chief princes' in a passage where the princes seem to be angels given responsibility for care of the nations. The latter provides men with understanding by interpreting visions.

The Old Testament writers used a whole range of ideas about angels. Many scholars think that belief in angels became more widespread during and after the exile, when the Jews were particularly aware of God's glory, and believed that He would approach men through intermediaries. If we attempt to summarize the ideas involved in the belief in angels, we could say that they are normally thought to live with the LORD in heaven (Gen. 28.12; 1 Kings 22.19; Neh. 9.6). This belief implies that they are spiritual, not physical beings. As spiritual beings they were thought to be present at the creation of the world, and to have rejoiced to see it brought into being (Job 38.4–7). The Jews accepted that Angels were free to come and go upon earth in the service of the LORD (Gen. 28.12; Job 1.7), and that they were the messengers of the LORD. We have noticed that the name 'angel' comes from a word meaning messenger. Old Testament writers say that when angels appear to men they look like men (Jos. 5.13; Dan. 9.21). Sometimes they make their presence known through dreams (Gen. 28.12), but not always (Judg. 13.3). In heaven they worship the LORD (Neh. 9.6; Ps. 97.7).

Some writers suggest that angels are not always obedient to the LORD. There is an ancient myth about the sons of God taking human wives which expresses this idea (Gen. 6.2–4), and the idea is developed in the book of Job: 'Can man be pure before his Maker? Even . . . his angels he charges with error' (Job 4.18). The LORD 'judges those that are on high' (Job 21.22). He restores 'peace in his high heaven' (Job 25.2). To complete this group of ideas, we find in Isaiah 24.21: 'On that day the LORD will punish the hosts of heaven, in heaven.' It seems that these writers believed that one of the qualities of any spiritual being is the power to make decisions, and to choose ways of behaving. Even the angels can choose evil if they wish. This prepares the way for the development of ideas about Satan, which we study in a later section.

People today vary widely in their attitude to the existence of angels. Some take the view that, since biblical writers make use of the idea of angels, they must be a real part of the world which God has created. Others think that the biblical writers used the idea of angels to express something of the mystery of their own spiritual experiences, which today would be described in other ways. These people see the idea of angels as a way of expressing the majesty and glory of the LORD, and at the same time showing the immediate and personal nature of spiritual experience. They say that the biblical writers thought of God as so great, powerful, and holy that men could not see Him face to face and live, but that these writers also knew that God had made His loving purposes for mankind known to them for their good: they thought that this knowledge had reached men through the work of angels.

The closest parallel to meeting with angels which Christians of our own time experience, seems to be the pentecostal experience of the Holy Spirit. But this does not exclude the possibility of the existence of angels, since this area of our lives is so full of wonder and mystery that no pattern of words can be accepted as a full, precise, and final account of our experience of the nearness of God. It is perhaps pride which leads us to claim that human beings are the only spiritual creatures. God's creative activity need not be so limited. The existence of other fallen spiritual beings beside ourselves may help to explain the existence of evil which does not arise from human sin (see p. 124).

## STUDY SUGGESTIONS

WORDS

1. The prefix *omni* comes from the Latin for *all*. Can you suggest the meaning of each of the following words, which are sometimes used to describe some part of the nature of the LORD?
   Omnipotence     Omnipresence     Omniscience
2. We have used the word 'implies' several times so far in this book. Which two of the following words are nearest to it in meaning?
   assumes  contradicts  denies  shows  suggests  supposes

CONTENT

3. Why do writers of the Old Testament reject the idea that people should seek contact with the spirits of the dead?
4. The Hebrew Bible is divided into three sections: the Law, the Prophets, and the Writings. Do we find the idea of other spiritual beings sometimes called angels, in all three parts of the Old Testament? Give Bible references from this textbook to support your answer.

BIBLE

5. (a) Use a Concordance to discover where the plural 'spirits' is used in the Old Testament. What sorts of beings are referred to when the plural is used?
   (b) Give references to support your answer.
6. How would you explain the meaning of Psalm 82 in the light of all that has been said about angels in this section of the guide?

DISCUSSION

7. Some Christians believe that angels are imaginary. They think that writers of the Old Testament used the idea of angels to help them express certain ideas about the spiritual world, but that angels do not really exist.
   (a) What do you yourself believe about them?

(b) How would you try to persuade somebody else that what you believe is true?

8. How would you counsel a Christian who feels that spirits are having a powerful influence in his life? Should he be encouraged to ignore them, to worship them, to deny their existence, or what?

9. (a) Should we identify angels with the lesser gods of many other religions?
(b) Is there likely to be any difference in the patterns of worship used by those who believe in angels, compared with those used by people who accept the existence of lesser gods?

## THE ANGEL OF THE LORD

Some of the earliest writings of the Old Testament refer in a special way to the 'Angel of the LORD', or the 'Angel of God'. These phrases are not merely references to one of the LORD's messengers. As we read the passages concerned, we find that the angel *is* the LORD. For example, in the story of Hagar (Gen. 16.7–13) we read 'The angel of the LORD said . . .' (16.9, 11), and this is followed by the statement that Hagar, 'called the name of *the LORD who spoke to her*, "Thou art a God of Seeing"' (16.13). In the story of the proposed sacrifice of Isaac (Gen. 22.9–14) the angel of the LORD said 'you have not withheld your son, your only son, from *me*' (22.12). The writer was not saying that Abraham was worshipping an angel, he was using the word 'angel' as another way of referring to God. Abraham's caution showed that he feared God (22.12).

In the story of Jacob's life in the family of Laban we read, 'Then the angel of God said . . . "I am the God of Bethel"' (Gen. 31.11–13). When Jacob blessed Joseph he first used the name of God, and then at the climax he used the word 'angel' to describe the source of power for the fulfilment of the blessing (Gen. 48.15, 16). Gideon believed that it was as dangerous to see the angel of the LORD as it would be to see God Himself (Judg. 6.22–23; compare Exod. 33.20).

This special use of the idea of the angel of the LORD as representing God himself is not found in any of the later writings, where angels are carefully described as 'servants' of the LORD. But among the prophecies in the second half of the book of Zechariah the idea reappears, i.e. right at the end of the period of Old Testament writings (Zech. 12.8). The writer of this prophecy had said the greatest thing he could about the glory of the house of David. It would 'be like God'. The addition of 'like the angel of the LORD' confirms and explains the idea, it does not reduce the glory attributed to the house of David. If anything it emphasizes that David will be like God in his dealings with human beings.

We need to understand the full meaning of the title 'angel of the LORD'. It cannot have meant that some angel was so identified with the LORD that he carried all God's power and authority. This does not fit the way in which the title is used. To repeat what we said earlier: the angel *is* the LORD.

The explanation seems to be that the writers who used this title wanted to preserve the wonder and glory of the LORD. God is separate from and greater than the whole universe in His power and glory. To use a technical term: God is 'transcendent'. Yet according to all these stories God was present with His people, with Hagar, Abraham, Jacob, etc. He was not simply represented by some lesser being, He was Himself present and available to the people. To use another technical term: God was 'immanent'. It was difficult for the writers of the Old Testament to express these two facts at one and the same time: God is transcendent, God is immanent. So they used the idea of the angel of the LORD to express God's presence with his people, and the title 'LORD' to express his separateness and glory.

In Christian thought the Holy Spirit is the person of the Godhead present with his people. In the Old Testament also, writers came to use the term 'Spirit of the LORD' when they tried to express the presence of the LORD with His people. It expresses this idea better than the term the 'angel of the LORD', because it includes a recognition of the power set free in the lives of men by the working of the Spirit. Yet the Spirit, as described in the Old Testament was less personal in character than the Angel of the LORD was believed to be. For this reason, too, writers used the term 'spirit' more often as they increasingly emphasized the idea of God's unity.

## SATAN

*Satan* is a Hebrew word meaning an 'adversary': someone who opposes another's plans. The word can be used quite simply about one man opposing another. The Philistines feared that David would become their 'adversary' (1 Sam. 29.4). David's own servants became his 'adversaries' when they advised him to do something he believed to be wrong (2 Sam. 19.22). Foreign rulers were 'adversaries' of Israel in the time of Solomon (1 Kings 11.14, 23, 25). According to the writer of the book of Kings, human 'adversaries' were *raised up* by God, who could also give a time of peace (1 Kings 5.4).

The word Satan was also used as a title for an official in the law-courts of Israel, whose duty was to find fault with people and show that they were doing wrong, rather like the 'prosecutor' in some modern courts (Ps. 109.6). The writer of this Psalm believed that his adversaries were themselves wicked men (see Ps. 109.4 where 'accuse' comes from the same Hebrew word *satan*).

The angel of the LORD also could be an 'adversary' e.g. in preventing Balaam from cursing the Israelites (Num. 22.22). God's actions were not always a blessing, He could also cause evil (Amos. 3.6 where NEB has 'disasters', Job. 2.11). But He did so in order to oppose the corrupt will of man. When Saul turned against the LORD, and was disobedient (1 Sam. 15.26) 'an evil spirit from the LORD tormented him' (1 Sam. 16.14, 15). This expresses Saul's sense of frustration and anger when God punished him because he had turned away from serving the LORD.

Similarly in 1 Kings 22.19–23, Micaiah describes a vision he had of God and the heavenly court of angels, in which they discussed how to oppose Ahab, who was leading Israel into evil ways. One of the angels offered to become a lying spirit to mislead the prophets, so that Ahab would be encouraged to fight in a battle in which he would be defeated and die. Notice that in this story God is pictured as permitting the deception, but not as responsible for suggesting it, or carrying it out. There is here the beginnings of the idea of a heavenly adversary belonging to the courts of God, and acting against men.

In 2 Samuel 24.1–14 the writer describes the LORD encouraging David to make a census of his people, and then condemning and punishing him for doing so. Probably the writer felt that since God was able to make use of David's wrong-doing as an opportunity to punish Israel, He must have prepared the situation by prompting David's action. But the writer of 1 Chronicles 21.1, tells the story with a very significant change. He says, 'Satan stood up against Israel, and incited David to number Israel.' Here again we have the idea of a heavenly being serving the LORD's purpose, but doing things that God himself would not do. In this verse the word *satan* is used without a definite article, and this may indicate that it stands as a personal name rather than as meaning 'the Adversary'.

The prologue to the book of Job provides the fullest description of Satan in the Old Testament. According to this account he belongs among the 'sons of God', i.e. the angels (Job 1.6). He has a work to do in which he serves the LORD, and must from time to time report to God on the results of his work. His work is to search out men's sins, and to bring cases against them in the heavenly courts. He has freedom to take action in the world to test the reactions of men to various kinds of trouble and suffering. But he must have God's approval for what he does. In the story, Job suffers the loss of all his possessions and his children, and later becomes seriously ill. Satan causes all this in order to test Job's faithfulness, and is convinced that Job will fail the test. Job does not know why he is suffering, but he is sure that in some way God is involved. He is not the victim of forces that are wholly evil and entirely opposed to God.

In Zechariah 3.2 we find a similar picture of the activity of Satan.

'The prologue to the book of Job provides the fullest description of Satan in the Old Testament' (p. 50). But Satan is never described in physical terms. Many Christians have heard that Satan has horns, cloven feet, and a tail; but these ideas are not found in the Bible. They seem to come from pagan ideas of demons or gods of evil, such as the demon Pazuzu, shown here in a small statue from Mesopotamia.

51

But there the LORD rebukes him for taking too much delight in the punishment of sinners. God intends to show mercy to Joshua, and Satan is not allowed to prevent this. The Old Testament never shows Satan as acting independently or in opposition to the LORD. It is in the Apocrypha that a writer suggests a link between Satan and the serpent mentioned in Genesis 3, as the source of temptation and the cause of men's fall (Wisdom of Solomon 2.23, 24).

The importance of this study of the development of ideas about Satan is that none of the Old Testament writers make the mistake of suggesting that evil is caused by some eternally independent being, acting at all times in opposition to the LORD. They have firmly grasped the fact that *all* things come from God, and then struggle with the problem of evil in a world which God created. The difficulty is resolved eventually in Jewish literature not included in the Old Testament (e.g. in *The Secrets of Enoch*) by supposing that one of the angels whom the LORD created has turned against Him, and is using his freedom to upset God's purposes. The Old Testament writers point to this idea without fully expressing it. Once it is expressed it gives cause for hope, because Satan is a creature of the LORD and cannot finally disrupt His purposes. Jesus used this understanding of Satan in His own teachings, e.g. Luke 10.18.

## STUDY SUGGESTIONS

WORDS

1. Which of the following words are associated with the idea of immanence, and which with the idea of transcendence?
   almighty  available  creator  eternal  helpful  loving  near perfect  personal  separate
2. Which of the following words is nearest in meaning to the word 'Adversary' as it is used in the Old Testament?
   brawler  competitor  opponent  revolutionary  rival

CONTENT

3. What is the difference between the Angel of the LORD described in Genesis, and the angels mentioned in the Psalms?
4. What evidence is there in the Old Testament that the Israelites believed Satan was one of the angels?

BIBLE

5. One way to speak of the LORD as transcendent is to call Him *almighty*. What activities of God are associated with the use of this name in the *Torah*? (For the meaning of *Torah* see Vol. 2, p. 16.)
6. (a) Use a Concordance to discover what the Old Testament writers say about evil spirits.

(b) In what ways is this different from ideas about evil spirits in any traditional religion with which you are familiar?

DISCUSSION

7. Some Christians say that belief in 'Satan' is part of the Jewish religion which Christians should reject. They say that people are glad to have someone to blame for their failures and sin.
   What do you think about this? Give full reasons for your opinion.
8. (a) Does the word 'evil' always mean 'wicked, or sinful'? What other meanings can you suggest?
   (b) How does your answer affect your understanding of Amos 3.6?

# CHAPTER 3

# Man

## MAN'S CREATION AND DESTINY

Thou hast made him little less than God,
and dost crown him with glory and honour.
(Psalm 8.5)

The writer to the Hebrews in the New Testament quotes this verse
from the Septuagint, but in his words man is 'for a little while lower
than the angels' (Heb. 2.7). We have already seen that in the Old
Testament the angels were sometimes called gods (p. 45), and this
probably explains the change made in the Greek translation. But
whichever version we follow, this Psalmist teaches that man has a
central place in the LORD's work of creation.

This belief is supported by the stories of Creation in Genesis. According to the J-traditions (Gen. 2.4–25), God made man first, and then
made everything else for man's use. According to the P-traditions
(Gen. 1.1—2.4), God created man at the climax of creation, on the
sixth day. God made man in His own image (Gen. 1.26), and gave him
dominion over all living things (Gen. 1.28).

The two stories give different accounts of when man was made, and
how he was made. The editor who included both stories in preparing
the book of Genesis, clearly did not feel that there was any real conflict
between the ideas of the two stories. He was not trying to give precise
details of the order of creation, or to describe exactly the way the world
was made. He believed that both stories taught the same basic truths:
that it was the LORD who created the world, and that the LORD gave
mankind a central place in creation.

Those Christians today who believe that archaeology and biology
have provided important clues about how the world was made, still
believe in these basic truths. They try to describe creation in the light
of this new knowledge, and they teach that the LORD caused these
things to happen, and made man the highest outcome of evolution.
In the future men will discover even more about the way creation
happened, but this will not hinder Christians from recognizing the
work of the LORD, and wondering at His care and concern for man
(Ps. 8.3, 4).

The two stories of creation involve important beliefs about the nature
and destiny of man. We must study these now.

54

## 1. MAN AND CREATION

Both stories recognize that *man is part of creation*, and that he is closely related to the physical world and to animals.

In the J-traditions both animals and men are described as 'living creatures', in some ways they are the same sort of being (Gen. 2.7, 19). Man was made of 'dust from the ground', and animals were formed 'out of the ground' (Gen. 2.7, 19). This implies a close physical relationship between animals and humans, which is fully supported by the scientific evidence of evolution and the origin of living beings. Both animals and men have in them 'the breath of life', which in the Bible means a vitality that comes from God (Gen. 2.7; 7.22).

In the P-traditions a special Hebrew word is used to describe God's work as creator. The same word is used to describe how He made the heavens and the earth (Gen. 1.1), living creatures of the seas, and birds (Gen. 1.21), and mankind (Gen. 1.27). There is no separate word to describe the origin of mankind. Human beings are part of creation, like all other things.

## 2. MAN AND OTHER CREATURES

Both traditions recognize that *man is greater than other created things*.

In the J-traditions man is at the centre of the whole story of creation. God prepared the garden of Eden as man's home (Gen. 2.8). God made animals and gave man authority to name them. In Hebrew thought, anyone who knows the name of a living creature has power over that creature. So the significance of Genesis 2.19 is that man has power over animals and other living creatures. Woman shares man's authority, because she shares his own essential nature, and is not a separate independent creation (Gen. 2.22).

In the P-traditions God gave mankind, both male and female, dominion over other living creatures (Gen. 1.26). Dominion means 'the right to rule', and so in God's purposes man rules over the other created beings. This too is supported by the history of human development as compared with that of other living creatures. God also instructed man to become master of the physical world in which he lived: 'fill the earth and subdue it' (Gen. 1.28).

## 3. MAN AND GOD

Both traditions recognize that *man has a special relationship with God*.

In the J-traditions the Lord God *breathed* into man's nostrils the breath of life (Gen. 2.7). This suggests a close personal relationship in creation, as a contrast to the statement that the LORD God *formed* every beast, etc. (Gen. 2.19). The LORD God talked with man, and shared a knowledge of His purposes with him (Gen. 2.17).

In the P-traditions, God told man how to serve him (Gen. 1.28–30). But the special relationship is expressed by the statement that: 'God created man in his own image, in the image of God he created him' (Gen. 1.27).

Scholars differ greatly in their interpretation of the phrase *the image of God*. Some believe that the writer intended an actual physical likeness between God and man. They draw our attention to the fact that God is often described in the Old Testament as though he were a man. God is said to have hands (1 Sam. 5.11), feet (Gen. 3.8), and a face (Gen. 32.30). He is said to have ears and eyes to know things (2 Kings 19.16), and an arm to achieve His purposes (Isa. 52.10). He is also described as doing human things: laughing (Ps. 2.4; 37.13), smelling (Gen. 8.21), and whistling (Isa. 7.18). These scholars suppose that the people of Old Testament times thought that God was in some senses a super-man.

No doubt some of the Israelites did take these ideas literally. But this does not provide a satisfactory explanation for the meaning of the phrase 'image of God'. The term comes from one of the later written sources, known as 'P', which belongs to the time of the exile or afterwards. Long before that time the Israelites knew that God could not be represented by any physical likeness (Exod. 20.4). The evidence of the Bible, and of archaeology, is that no image of the LORD was ever used in Israel, not even an image in human shape.

All the verses mentioned above in which God is described in human ways are intended to express spiritual realities about His life, knowledge, and activity. The Israelites had no better words to express the truth about God than the words they used to describe the life, knowledge, and activities of human beings. They used such words because they wanted to share their knowledge of the ways of God, and this was the only way they could do it.

God Himself had used this way of expressing the truth about His personal reality and activity. He appeared to men in dreams and visions as a man (e.g. Isa. 6.1; Dan. 7.9) in order that they might understand the things He wanted to reveal to them. But these physical appearances were only a way of making people aware of His presence and power. They did not necessarily imply that God is actually man-shaped. He is something more wonderful and lovely than the best of men.

So the use of the phrase 'image of God' means something different from a belief that man and God share the same physical appearance. But scholars who look for another meaning to this phrase do not all agree in the way it should be interpreted.

(a) Some believe it is another way of speaking of the authority which God has given to man. Just as God has dominion, so man has dominion.

'Scholars differ greatly in their interpretation of the phrase 'the image of God'.
Some believe that the writer intended an actual physical likeness between God
and man' (p. 56). The Egyptians believed that there was a close relationship between
the Pharaohs and their gods. In an inscription inside the pyramid of Unis at Sakkara
the dead Pharaoh is spoken to in these words: 'Thy arm is Atum, thy shoulders are
Atum, thy belly is Atum, thy back is Atum, thy rear is Atum, thy legs are Atum, thy
face is Anubis.' Clearly the Egyptians supposed there was an actual physical likeness
between the Pharaoh Unis and the god Atum.

57

(b) Some believe that the phrase means that man is God's representative in the created universe, and that his dominion springs from the fact that he has been given a share of God's authority.

(c) Some believe that man has been made in the image of God in the sense that he shares God's moral nature: being able to distinguish between right and wrong, and able to choose and do what is good.

Probably all these ideas are included in this phrase, but one way of expressing its meaning covers them all: *man is spiritual, as God is spiritual*. So far as we know, no other creature on this planet combines in his nature the two qualities of physical and spiritual in the way that man does. Because of this spiritual nature of man we can rightly use human terms to describe God. Eventually it was the spiritual nature of man that made it possible for God to become incarnate, to be born as a man in Christ Jesus.

4. GOD'S CONCERN FOR HUMAN BEINGS

Both traditions recognize *God's concern for the well-being of mankind*. There is a positive purpose and value in God's creation of human beings. In both the creation stories this belief is expressed in the commands that God gives to man (Gen. 2.16; 1.28). The J-tradition, which was written long before the P-tradition, goes on to describe how mankind acted against the purposes of God, and brought trouble into the world. We shall study the nature and results of sin in a later chapter. It is sufficient here to notice that God intended man to have life, and life that involved a personal relationship with Himself. The commandments in the creation stories imply this relationship. We shall study the Israelites' understanding of death later, but we must notice here that what they hoped for was life with the continuing possibility of relationship with God.

## STUDY SUGGESTIONS

WORDS

1. Which of the following definitions best matches the meaning of the word 'destiny' in the heading to this section?
   (a) A goal to be reached, a final event to be worked for.
   (b) A way of life that is the real reason for living.
   (c) Something that cannot be avoided, which is certain to happen.
2. A man may see an image of himself by looking at any of the following things. Which one of them shows an image similar to the image of God in man?
   his child    his mirror    his photograph    his portrait
   his sculpture

CONTENT

3. What four ideas about the relationship between man and God are found in the two biblical accounts of creation?
4. (a) How was man made, according to the two stories of creation?
(b) In what way if any, does the difference between the two accounts affect our belief in what the Bible says about creation?

BIBLE

5. Dominion means 'the right to rule' (p. 55).
Who or what may have the right to rule, according to the following verses, and in what way is their dominion limited?
(a) Psalm 72.8   (b) Micah 4.8   (c) Psalm 19.13   (d) Daniel 7.14
6. (a) Make a list of the verses in the Old Testament where the word 'image' is used, but do not include those verses in which it stands for an idol, or an object that is worshipped.
(b) Can you replace the word 'image' by the words 'spiritual likeness' in all the verses you have listed, and get good sense from them? How does this evidence help you to understand the idea of man being made in the image of God?

DISCUSSION

7. (a) Make as full a list as you can of the characteristics which man shares with animals.
(b) Is man always more capable in all these things than the animals?
(c) Do some animals possess greater powers than men in some aspects of life?
Give examples to support your answers to (b) and (c).
8. (a) In what ways do the theories of evolution help to explain the relationship between man and other living creatures?
(b) What difference do they make, if any, to our understanding of the relationship between man and God?

## MAN'S NATURE

All the writers of the Old Testament were concerned with the life of mankind. They described the thoughts, feelings, and actions of men in many different ways. Scholars have found evidence to support several different views of man's essential nature. Some speak of man as having three parts: body, soul, and spirit. Some prefer to describe the two parts of man: physical and spiritual. Most agree that whatever parts of human nature are distinguished in Israelite thought, the most important belief is that human life is a unity, and that the various parts of are neither in conflict, nor entirely independent of each other.

The difficulty in describing the exact nature of the Old Testament ideas about man comes from the fact that in Hebrew, as in other languages, many words have more than one meaning. Often their meanings overlap, so that it is not possible to say that this word means one thing, and that word means something quite different. At times they bear similar meanings, and at other times they express quite different ideas.

In the study of the Old Testament, scholars do not always agree about the meaning the writer was giving to a word in a particular verse, and as a result they translate it in different ways (see p. 38).

The work of discovering a recognizable pattern of Israelite thought about man is impossible for most people, because the English and other translations of the Bible do not show what Hebrew words lie behind the interpretation given.

1. The same Hebrew word is translated in different Bible versions and in different passages in any one version by different English words. For example, the ordinary Hebrew word for heart is in many cases translated 'heart' (Gen. 6.5, etc.), but it is also given as 'accord' (Ps. 83.5), 'sense' (Prov. 6.32), and 'understanding' (Job 36.5), etc.

2. Different Hebrew words are sometimes translated by the same English word. The word 'mind' may be used in our Bibles as a translation of various Hebrew words which are usually translated as heart, soul, spirit, etc.

Some attempt must be made to bring order out of what seems like confusion. So let us discover what we can about Israelite thought by using the two-part division of human nature suggested by the creation stories and often used by Christians: physical and spiritual. But we do this chiefly as a matter of convenience. It was the Greek philosophers who developed the idea that human beings are made up of a number of quite separate parts. The Israelites themselves were deeply aware of the unity of human nature, and we shall find that the two groups of ideas are closely interrelated in the thought of Old Testament writers.

### I. MAN'S PHYSICAL NATURE

The ordinary Hebrew word for 'body' is not used very much in the Old Testament. Where it is used, it can, like the English word 'body' mean living people (Gen. 47.18; Neh. 9.37), or corpses (1 Sam. 31.10, 12; Ps. 110.6). It can be used of the carcases of dead animals (Jud. 14.8). It can also be used of the physical appearances of spiritual beings seen in a vision (Dan. 10.6; Ezek. 1.11, 23).

Much more often the Hebrew word for *flesh* is used. This can describe the material of which animal (Lev. 4.11) and human (Lev. 13.10) bodies are made. It also describes the closeness of human relationships (Gen. 2.23; 37.27, etc.). It can be used to express the weakness of created beings, including men, in comparison with the almighty power of God (Gen. 6.3; Job 34.14–15). But there is no suggestion in the Old Testament that flesh is corrupt (contrast Rom. 7.18). All flesh, (i.e. all created beings) shall see glory of the LORD (Isa. 40.5).

The Israelites did not know much about the workings of the human body. The brain is never mentioned in the Old Testament, even though it controls the activities of the body. Muscles and sinews are described as merely joining the parts of the body together (Ezek. 37.8). There is no suggestion that movement depends on their use. But the Israelites did know about some of the internal organs of the body, and supposed that these controlled people's mental and emotional life.

Chief among these organs is the *heart*. The Hebrew word can be used to mean a person's physical heart (Ps. 22.14). But it was also used to describe the source of appetite (Ps. 104.15) and the centre for emotions (Exod. 4.14; Ps. 55.4). The Israelites believed that thought takes place in the heart: and that it was the place for understanding (Isa. 6.10) and memory (see Deut. 30.1 where 'mind' translates the Hebrew word for heart). They believed that a man's will is formed in his heart (Prov. 6.18), and that character comes from it (Ps. 24.4; 1 Kings 9.4), even bad character (Deut. 8.14; 15.7).

Old Testament writers also used other words which mean various internal organs of the body. But the translators of the RSV in nearly all cases used 'heart' or 'soul' where these words are used in the Hebrew scriptures, because at the time when the RSV was prepared it was not considered polite to speak of the bowels, the womb, etc. as freely as the Israelites did. This hides the different shades of meaning in Hebrew between the various organs and the purposes they were thought to fulfil. So we must take brief notice of these differences here.

The belly was thought of as the source of a person's willpower. (Job 15.35), and the kidneys as the source of conscience (Ps. 16.7; 73.21; Prov. 23.16). Grief came from the liver (Lam. 2.11), and compassion from the bowels (Isa. 16.11; Jer. 31.20) or the womb (Isa. 63.15; Ps. 77.9). Most scholars agree that these ideas arose out of physical experience. The Israelites recognized the physical feelings which go with strong emotions of various kinds: joy, grief, shame, desire, etc., and they supposed that these feelings showed the sources of the emotions, mostly in the abdomen.

These ideas illustrate the Israelites' belief that the physical, emotional, and spiritual natures of man are closely related. It is interesting to note that modern doctors and psychologists are more and more stressing this interrelation between body and mind. Physical ill-health can affect the mind, and mental distress can affect the body. Healing must involve the whole man. Such ideas are closely related to the Israelites' ideas, and partly arise from similar human experiences.

We shall see later, however, that these beliefs deeply affected the Israelites' understanding of death. They did not imagine that the mental and spiritual part of human nature could have any separate life, with any real experience or purpose, outside the body. *Sheol* (i.e. the underworld, to which they believed that people go after death), was regarded as a place of shadowy existence, to be avoided as long as possible.

## 2. MAN'S SPIRITUAL NATURE

Two important Hebrew words need careful study here if we are to understand the ideas of the Old Testament writers.

1. *Soul*: The Hebrew word usually translated as 'soul' is used about 700 times in the Old Testament. Apart from 'soul', the most frequent translations for this word in the RSV are 'life' (Gen. 19.17; Jer. 11.21), 'person' (Deut. 10.22; Jer. 43.6), and 'self, myself, etc.' (Job 18.4; Isa. 46.2). These various translations show that this Hebrew word meant the active, living part of a person's nature. The same word is used in the phrase 'living being' in Genesis 2.7, where it is translated 'being'. And it is also used in relation to animals in Genesis 1.21, 24, where it is translated 'creature'.

Although the Israelites referred in this way to a person's soul, as well as to the physical body: 'the LORD will destroy both soul and body' (Isa. 10.18), they did not distinguish clearly, as the Greeks did, between the soul and the bodily organs, so that either could be described as the source of emotions, such as hate (2 Sam. 5.8; Ps. 105.25) or joy (Isa. 61.10; 66.14). The Israelites' great desire was that the LORD would deliver their souls from death (e.g. Ps. 22.20). At death, they thought, the soul leaves the body (Gen. 35.18), and goes to *Sheol*, the place of the dead (Ps. 86.13). Perhaps the best word in modern English to express the idea of the soul is 'personality': the thing which makes each person an individual different from all others, the self which departs at death so that only a body remains.

2. *Spirit*: The Hebrew word usually translated as 'spirit' is used about 400 times in the Old Testament, but it is used about God, and about other spiritual beings, as well as about human beings. It is not always easy to be sure which sense is intended in any particular verse of the Old Testament. The translators of the RSV have used a capital S for the word where they believe that it refers to God. In some passages in the Old Testament, however, scholars are uncertain whether the Spirit of God or the spirit of man is intended. The close relationship between the two makes it especially difficult to distinguish between them.

Apart from 'spirit', the commonest translations of this word as used in the Old Testament are 'wind' (Gen. 8.1; Isa. 7.2), and 'breath'

(1 Kings 17.17; Job 27.3). These translations suggest that spirit is the driving force of life, providing energy for action, and enabling body and soul together to have life (Job 27.3). Man's spirit is a gift from God (Isa. 42.5), and if God withdrew the gift, man would cease to exist (Job 34.14–15). Living things die when God takes away their breath (Ps. 104.29).

God's Spirit enables people to achieve many things which they could not achieve without it. His presence with human beings enriches their life, and enables the human spirit to reach its fullest powers. The Spirit of God enabled Bezalel to be a skilled craftsman (Exod. 31.3), and Samson to exercise his great strength (Judg. 14.6). By the same power the Judges defeated the enemies of Israel (Judg. 3.10), David ruled in Israel (1 Sam. 16.13), and the prophets spoke in God's name (Isa. 61.1). We have already noticed that the Old Testament emphasis on the Unity of God prevented the Israelites from recognizing the fully personal nature of the Holy Spirit. But they could not ignore the difference made to the lives of some of their leaders when the Spirit of God 'clothed' (Judg. 6.34; 2 Chron. 24.20 see RSV footnotes), 'filled' (Exod. 31.3), or 'poured upon' (Isa. 44.3) them.

The spirit of man is not always pure. Human beings are described as erring in spirit (Isa. 29.24), or having a spirit of confusion (Isa. 19.14), harlotry (Hos. 4.12), or unfaithfulness (Ps. 78.8). But the LORD can revive their spirit (Isa. 57.15), and put a new and right spirit within them (Ps. 51.10). The presence of God's own Spirit makes this possible (Isa. 11.2) and in fullest power it produces in His people a spirit of wisdom, understanding, counsel, might, knowledge, and fear of the LORD.

## STUDY SUGGESTIONS

WORDS

1. Words describing parts of the body often have more than one meaning. Can you provide, for each pair of words below, the name of the part of the body which links together the two ideas they suggest, e.g. 'see' and 'needle' would be linked by 'eye'.
   (a) Stand and length
   (b) grip and employee
   (c) taste and language
   (d) pump and emotions
   (e) digestion and appetite.
2. 'The two-part division of human nature often used by Christians: physical and spiritual' (p. 60).
   Which two of the following words would best help describe the meaning of the word 'part' in the sentence?
   component  detachable  distinct  integral  scattered  separate

# MAN

CONTENT

3. Why did the Israelites connect strong emotions with various internal organs of the body?

4. What is the difference in meaning between 'soul' and 'spirit', according to the use of these words in the Old Testament?

BIBLE

5. According to Genesis 9.4 a person's soul is in his blood. This belief gave the Israelites a special horror of bloodshed, and they thought this crime should be severely punished. Illustrate this fact by examples from 2 Samuel.

6. (a) If your Library possesses a copy of Young's *Analytical Concordance to the Bible*, look up the word 'mind' and discover how many different Hebrew words are translated by this one English word.

   (b) Make a list of the more usual translations of these Hebrew words.

   (c) Is there a special Hebrew word which must normally be translated 'mind'?

DISCUSSION

7. In what ways does the evidence studied in this chapter support the idea accepted by some scholars that the Israelites believed that human beings are composed of two parts: physical and spiritual? Give Bible references to support your answer.

8. How would you describe the relationship between the Spirit of the Lord, and the spirit of man?

9. (a) Give examples of ways in which the methods of science as applied to the study of human nature support the Israelites' ideas about the physical and the spiritual aspects of man.

   (b) Which branches of science are concerned especially with the study of human nature, and how are they related to the physical and the spiritual aspects of it?

10. Any religion or philosophy which attempts to explain the meaning and significance of human life must also attempt to describe the nature of man.

    (a) Describe as fully as you can what is believed about the nature of man in any religious teaching known to you, other than Christian teaching.

    (b) In what respects is this belief different from the ideas held by the Israelites? How far do you think such differences make it difficult for people of other religions to understand the teaching contained in the Bible?

# BIRTH, LIFE, DEATH

The writers of the Old Testament had quite a lot to say about the origin of individual human beings, the part they are able to play in the life of the nation, and their experiences after death. So now we must look at this sequence of ideas in order to complete our study of the nature of man.

## 1. BIRTH

The Israelites believed that conception is a gift from the LORD, which He gives or withholds as He wishes. This idea is most fully expressed in the story of Jacob and his two wives. Leah bore many children, but Rachel seemed to be barren. She complained to Jacob, but he replied 'Am I in the place of God, who has withheld from you the fruit of the womb'? (Gen. 30.1; compare 29.31). The same idea underlies the stories of barren women who pray for children, and receive them as a result, e.g. the mother of Esau and Jacob (Gen. 25.21), and the mother of Samuel (1 Sam. 1.19, 20). But normal conception is also often described as a gift from God (Gen. 4.1; Ruth 4.13, etc.).

Because the Israelites knew none of the physiological reasons for the development of the foetus in the womb, they believed it to be a mystery directly controlled by the LORD (Job 31.15; Ps. 119.73). They described the way the LORD works to make each human being, though in very general terms which suggest that the physical as well as the spiritual side of human nature develops under His control (Ps. 139.13–15; Job 10.8–11). But there are verses which suggest that it is the spiritual part of human nature, especially, which comes from God in the birth of each child. According to Ecclesiastes 11.5 it is 'how the spirit comes to the bones' which is the greatest mystery. The LORD 'made our souls' (Jer. 38.16), 'and formed the spirit of man within him' (Zech. 12.1). He 'fashions the hearts of them all' (Ps. 33.15). The prophet Jeremiah believed that he had been chosen to serve God before he was born, and even that God had made him for that very purpose (Jer. 1.5).

## 2. ROLE IN LIFE

We have already noticed that the Israelites believed that the LORD was active within the events of history (see p. 29). We saw that the LORD often brought his purposes to fulfilment through the obedience of men who responded to His call: e.g. Abraham, Moses, David, etc. Such men believed that they had a special part to play in the history of God's people.

But they knew that they were chosen to enable the whole nation to fulfil its role within God's purposes. At the centre of these purposes was the LORD's intention that the Israelites should know Him (Hos. 6.6). Some of the prophets expressed God's anger and distress that His people did not know Him (Hos. 4.1; 5.4; Isa. 1.3; Jer. 4.22). The Law was intended to show the Israelites what God wanted from His people, and so to reveal the heart and mind of God. But 'those who handled the law did not know me' (Jer. 2.8). These same prophets looked forward to the time when God's people would know their LORD (Hos. 2.20). 'I will be their God, and they shall be my people. And no longer shall each man teach his neighbour and each his brother saying "Know the LORD", for they shall all know me, from the least of them to the greatest, says the LORD' (Jer. 31.33, 34). Here is God's purpose for every human life in Israel, and for His chosen nation within the world. The prophets believed that eventually it would be recognized as the role and purpose of all mankind (Isa. 2.3).

In order to reach this goal the LORD chose people to serve Him, and to do important things for Him. Abraham was chosen to establish a new family, and lead them towards their new home. Moses was chosen to rescue the Israelites from Egypt, and to bring them to God at Sinai. Joshua was chosen to lead the people into Palestine, and to help them settle in their new home. So one by one the leaders came, did their service, and departed. Each fulfilled a special role, a significant part of God's plans for His people.

Each of these men needed special qualities and abilities to fulfil the role that he was given. How were they equipped for their work? Did God search out from among the people somebody who possessed the necessary qualities? Did God endow His leaders with special qualities, which they would not have possessed as part of their natural and personal characteristics apart from God's special gift at the time of their call? Or is there some other explanation of their ability to do His will, and so fulfil the role He gave them?

We can find the answer to these questions by looking at stories which tell of the choice of new leaders, and especially those in which the person chosen doubted his ability to do the work that God gave him. The story of the call of Moses is given in Exodus 3—4. Moses felt inadequate for his work: 'Who am I that I should go to the Pharaoh'? (Exod. 3.11). God's answer was 'I will be with you'. The presence of the LORD would make all the difference. With God's help he would be able to do his duty. Later in the story Moses again raised doubts: 'Oh, my LORD, I am not eloquent . . . I am slow of speech and tongue' (Exod. 4.10). He assessed his own natural ability, and felt that he lacked the qualities needed for this work: 'either heretofore, or since thou hast spoken to thy servant'. God's presence had not altered that. The LORD's reply was 'Who has made man's mouth. . . . Is it not I?'

'I will be their God and they shall be my people.... They shall all know me, from the least to the greatest.... Here is God's purpose for all mankind' (p. 66).

A worker at his lathe in Hong Kong, a Japanese farmer's wife, the President of an African republic, Guatemalan children—in what ways do you think all these people, 'from the least to the greatest', will be affected by coming to know God, and His purposes for themselves and each other as His people?

(Exod. 4.11). Moses had forgotten that God was his creator, and knew what abilities he possessed better than Moses knew them himself. The LORD would enable him to use his hidden resources of speech in a way that Moses himself had never used them before.

Similar ideas are expressed in other parts of the Old Testament. When David was chosen to be king, the LORD told Samuel: 'the LORD sees not as man sees; man looks on the outward appearance, but the LORD looks on the heart' (1 Sam. 16.7). God is able to see what a man is capable of becoming, not merely what he is already. Seven of Jesse's sons were not properly equipped for such responsibilities, but David was, even though he was the youngest among them. The LORD knew where to send Samuel to find the one he wanted. He had provided Himself a king among Jesse's sons (1 Sam. 16.1).

Jeremiah's call began with the idea that God had been involved in his creation as an individual in his mother's womb. He had been equipped for the work of a prophet from his conception (Jer. 1.5). Jeremiah doubted his own ability, as he felt too young and inexperienced to be a prophet (Jer. 1.6). But the LORD promised to be with him to enable him to do His work (Jer. 1.8). The inborn qualities of Jeremiah would come to maturity through service in fellowship with the LORD.

These examples of the way in which God equips men for service will help us to understand the other calls to service which are described in the Old Testament. They cover a wide range of activities, involving all the leaders who were thought to be serving the LORD in some special role: patriarchs (e.g. Abraham, Gen. 12.1–3), judges (e.g. Gideon, Judg. 6.14), priests (Num. 18.6), prophets (e.g. Amos, Amos 7.15), craftsmen (2 Chron. 2.13, 14), musicians (1 Chron. 15.22). In fact the writer of the books of Chronicles recognized God's call as underlying the work of 'every willing man who has skill for any kind of service' (1 Chron. 28.21).

### 3. DEATH

The Israelites accepted death as part of the normal human experience. They referred to the 'common death of all men' (Num. 16.29). A psalmist asked, 'What man can live and never see death?', expecting the answer 'no one' (Ps. 89.48). The death of an important man served to mark the date when something happened. Notice the mention of death in the first verse of Joshua, Judges, 2 Samuel, and 2 Kings. They knew that death could result from natural causes, such as drinking dirty water (2 Kings 2.19–22) or eating the wrong things (2 Kings 4.38–41). They believed that certain crimes should be punished by death (see especially the Book of the Covenant, Exod. 20.22—23.33). They thought that God sent disease and famine to punish evil-doing, and that those who died were the evil-doers (Exod. 12.29; 2 Sam. 24.15).

The book of Deuteronomy describes the way of life that is pleasing to God, and explains that disobedience leads to death (Deut. 30.15–20). The Israelites also believed that God is able to deliver people from death (Pss. 68.20; 107.17–20), and that this provides them with a further opportunity to serve him (Pss. 9.13, 14; 56.13).

Yet even righteous people die eventually. Throughout most of the Old Testament the only privileges allowed to the righteous are long life, many children, and their memory preserved in Israel. The extra-ordinary ages to which the patriarchs are said to have lived were probably not their true ages, but simply a way of honouring the great men of the past. The writers seem to say, 'They were so righteous that God allowed them to have a very long life' (Gen. 25.7; 35.28; 47.28).

In other parts of the Old Testament the phrases 'a good old age' (Judg. 8.32; 1 Chron. 29.28), and 'full of days' (Job 42.17; 2 Chron. 24.15) are used to express the same idea: i.e. that long life is a gift of God to the righteous. Prayers were offered that God would prolong the life of the King (Pss. 61.6; 72.5). The unrighteous are 'cut off' (Lev. 20.3; 1 Kings 14.10; Ezek. 14.8). Children also were regarded as a reward for obedience (Deut. 7.13; Pss. 37.37; 127.3), a blessing not given to the unrighteous (Job 18.19). The memory of the righteous would remain for a long time among the living (Ps. 112.6; Prov. 10.7), while the unrighteous would be forgotten (Deut. 32.26; Ps. 34.16; Job 18.17).

These ideas are simply of blessings which hide the cruelty of death. At this stage there is no suggestion that the righteous would have a continuing personal life after death. Some of the Psalmists say quite bluntly that death is the end of personal existence (Pss. 39.13; 146.4; compare Job 7.21). Some biblical writers describe death as the reverse of creation. Man was made 'of dust from the ground', and received life from the breath of God (Gen. 2.7). If God withdraws the breath of life from a person, he dies (Ps. 104.29; 146.4; Job 12.10), and returns to the dust (Gen. 3.19; Job 34.14, 15; Eccles. 12.7). According to Ecclesiastes 12.7 'the spirit returns to God who gave it'. The writer did not intend to show the spirit as having independent life and sharing a personal relationship with God, he meant rather that the power for life had been withdrawn. The departure of the spirit was part of the break up and disappearance of the individual, as suggested by Job 34.14, 15.

Two stories in the early traditions of Israel, however, do suggest that certain people escaped the destruction involved in death. One was Enoch, who 'walked with God; and he was not, for God took him' (Gen. 5.24; compare Heb. 11.5, 6). The other was Elijah who 'went up by a whirlwind into heaven' (2 Kings 2.11). These stories express a growing desire among the Israelites to discover some future for the righteous. At this stage in the development of their ideas they could not believe that life was possible without survival of the complete person: both body and spirit. So they supposed that Enoch and Elijah had taken their physical bodies with them. Perhaps a similar idea lies beneath the traditions of the death of Moses, buried by God (Deut. 34.6). But even if so, later story-tellers were not convinced that it was possible for a man to escape in this way, and they simply recorded that 'no man knows the place of his burial'.

## 4. SHEOL

The first evidence for belief in some form of survival after death is found in the use of the Hebrew word *Sheol*. In some English versions this word is translated 'grave', but a careful study of the way the word is used in the Old Testament shows that it meant something different from the place where a body is buried. The translators of the RSV treat it as a special technical word with no exact English equivalent. They use the same word *Sheol*, simply transliterating from Hebrew into Roman script.

The belief about *Sheol* was approximately as follows: Sheol is situated in the depths of the earth (Ps. 63.9; 88.6). All the dead are gathered there (Isa. 14.9, 10) from every nation (Ezek. 32.18–32). The wicked go there after an early death (Ps. 9.17; 31.17) but the righteous men of Israel are there too (Gen. 37.35; 49.33). Sheol is a place of gloom and darkness (Job 10.21, 22). Those who are there survive in weakness (Isa. 14.10). 'There is no work or thought or knowledge or wisdom in Sheol' (Eccles. 9.10)—without a body activity is impossible. Job looked forward to Sheol as an escape from the sorrows and troubles of life: he believed he would have rest there (Job. 3.13, 17). But in fact it is a place of hopelessness (Job 17.13–16; Isa. 38.18). Those who live in Sheol are cut off from God (Ps. 88.10–12). They do not remember God (Ps. 6.5), nor praise him (Ps. 30.9; 115.17). Yet they do not escape from his authority and power (Ps. 139.8; Amos 9.2; Isa. 7.11). 'Sheol is naked before God' (Job 26.6). The worst thing about Sheol is that there is no escape, no return to life (2 Sam. 12.23; Job 14.12).

This picture of Sheol as the place of the dead is exactly what we would expect from the Israelites, when we remember that for them real life involved the whole person; body, soul, and spirit. When a man dies, his body is left in the grave, and only his bones survive (Gen. 50.25; Exod. 13.19). The personality of a man must therefore either disappear altogether or else linger on without the body as a means of life, and without the spirit as a power for life.

Yet the Israelites' belief in Sheol expressed a growing hope that man could expect something better beyond this life than mere decomposition.

This shadowy existence was preferable to no existence at all. Some of the Psalmists expressed their desire for the possibility of an escape from Sheol. Scholars disagree about the sort of escape: some think that the Psalmists were only speaking of a prolonged earthly life, but others think that they hoped for a real life after they left this world. Whichever view we take, it is clear that they based their hope on their knowledge of God's love for them, and His care and protection. They believed that God's love would continue, and that His care and protection could not possibly end by His delivering them into the life of Sheol. The Psalms which express this confidence in God are 16.10, 11; 17.15; 37.27–9; 49.15; 73.24–6. A similar idea seems to be expressed in Job 19.23–27, though in other parts of the same book we find the more traditional views of death and Sheol (but see footnote x in the RSV).

## 5. RESURRECTION

One final idea about the dead is mentioned briefly in writings that probably come from the latest period of Old Testament thought. This is the idea of resurrection: i.e. restoration to full human life after a period of death. This idea may have sprung from the three stories in the books of Kings about dead people who were raised to the life of this world again (1 Kings 17.17–24; 2 Kings 4.17–37; 13.21). But it does not seem that the idea was widely held among the Israelites, probably because they knew only too well about the decomposition of the body after death. They used the idea chiefly to describe the exile and return. Some of the prophets spoke of this as the death and resurrection of Israel (Hos. 6.1–3; Ezek. 37: the valley of dead bones).

There are only two passages in the Old Testament where the resurrection of dead people seems to be accepted as part of God's plan for mankind. Both these passages come from the apocalyptic writings, which emphasize God's power to achieve things that are impossible to men. Isaiah 26.19 describes a joyful resurrection for the righteous, although some scholars believe that this verse refers to the return from 'the death' of Exile (compare Hos. 6.1–3). Daniel 12.2 refers to resurrection for many, 'some to everlasting life, and some to shame'. Belief in some form of resurrection was necessary to fulfil the idea that true life must involve a complete human nature: body, soul, and spirit. But the writers of the Old Testament never tackled the problem that the human body is subject to decay and cannot keep its physical nature to all eternity. When we come to the New Testament, the changed body of the risen Christ gives some clue to the truth. St Paul expressed the answer by speaking of a spiritual body, suitable for the new form of life in heaven (1 Cor. 15.43–4).

# STUDY SUGGESTIONS

**WORDS**

1. Which two of the following words come nearest in meaning to the word 'role' as used in the phrase 'Role in Life' which is the heading of part of this section?
career   cast   character   function   living   part   policy

2. Different peoples have many different ideas about what happens to the dead. Each of the following words summarizes one of these ideas. What does each mean, and which, if any, did the writers of the Old Testament accept? Give Bible references where you can.
annihilation   reincarnation   resurrection   survival   translation
transmigration

**CONTENT**

3. What was the function of the Law in Israel? How well did it serve its purpose?

4. 'The inborn qualities of Jeremiah would come to maturity through service in fellowship with the LORD' (p. 68). Explain this sentence, and say whether you believe your own Call to serve the LORD should involve a similar development.

**BIBLE**

5. What did the writer of Ecclesiastes believe about death? (Vol. 2, p. 122–3 will help you).

6. Besides *Sheol* there is another word which has been transliterated from the Hebrew in the RSV: *Abaddon*. See Job 26.6; 28.22; 31.12; Ps. 88.11; Prov. 15.11; 27.20. Study these verses and see whether you can discover the meaning of the word. A Bible dictionary will help you.

**DISCUSSION**

7. (a) What pastoral advice would you give to a young married couple who were troubled because they seemed unable to have any children?
(b) What advice would you give them about prayer in this situation.

8. The name given to attempts to make contact with the spirits of the dead is 'spiritualism'.
(a) What are the traditional attitudes of most people in your country to spiritualism?
(b) In what way, if any does this conflict with biblical teaching?
(c) In what ways, if any, does the custom of some Churches of praying to the Virgin Mary, and to saints, differ from spiritualism?

9. (a) What do you yourself believe about life after death?
(b) What difficulties, if any, do you have in thinking about this subject?

# CHAPTER 4

# The Fall

## OBEDIENCE AND TEMPTATION

According to the writers of the Old Testament, God created human beings for a life of fellowship. Every new-born baby possesses the possibility of sharing a personal relationship with God, and of living in harmony with other human beings. This ideal is to be reached by an obedient response to the LORD, and a willingness to serve Him. If people in general, or individual men and women in particular, fail to reach the highest form of this relationship with God and with other men, they have 'fallen'. The 'Fall of Man' is the phrase which theologians use to express the fact that most people do not reach the highest experiences of the life which God has planned for them. The human race has failed to make proper use of the opportunities for living which God has provided.

### I. GOOD AND EVIL

In the writings of the Old Testament 'good' and 'evil' are related to God's purposes. Whatever leads to the fulfilment of God's will is *good*. It is in this sense that 'God saw everything that He had made, and behold it was very good' (Gen. 1.31). The whole creation is so planned that it makes possible the fulfilment of the LORD's purposes for mankind. Many things are described in the Old Testament as 'good': a good land (Exod. 3.8), good men (Prov. 12.2), good words (Isa. 39.8), etc. Each of these things is good because it helps to achieve God's will for His people.

Anything which goes against the will of God and hinders His purposes is *evil*. Many of the writers of the Old Testament describe the evil things which people do (Gen. 6.5; Isa. 13.11, etc.). These things are evil because they are contrary to the will of God. But the word 'evil' is also frequently used in the Old Testament to describe something which God has done (2 Kings 21.12; Neh. 13.17, 18: Jer. 4.6). It is not part of God's purpose to do evil to men. He does not act to defeat His own purposes. But there are times when he must punish rather than bless, in order to achieve his purposes. The suffering that is involved in punishment is what is meant when biblical writers talk about evil done by God. Its purpose is to correct sinful men. If people respond to punishment, then the LORD 'repents' of the evil, and returns to doing good (Exod. 32.14; Jer. 26.19). But this does not mean that God has acted unjustly, or with cruelty. There is never a time when He needs to repent of anything that is selfish, or unkind (1 Sam. 15.29). When writers say that He 'repents', they mean that He changes the way in which He is dealing with men, because a different approach will now enable Him to achieve His purposes for them.

## 2. FREEDOM TO CHOOSE

Human beings have freedom to choose between good and evil. Each person can either respond to God by obedience and service, or turn away from Him and do things contrary to His will. There are three Hebrew words which express a response which can be obedient, but may be the reverse.

1. One of these words means 'to choose' (Deut. 30.19; Ps. 119.30; Isa. 7.15).

2. Another word means 'to consent', and is always used to describe response to a command or suggestion. Almost always in the Old Testament this word is used in the negative, to describe an act of rebellion against God's purposes (Deut. 1.26; Ps. 81.11; Isa. 30.15).

3. The third word means to do something 'willingly' (Exod. 25.2; Judg. 5.2; Ps. 110.3).

It is clear from the use of these words that the Israelites believed that people have a choice in what they do. They are not driven to behave in the way they do by forces or powers outside themselves. Not even God compels response, even though His commandments are wise and good, and bring blessing.

The Israelites became aware of their freedom to choose, because they recognized the existence of evil. Even their great national heroes, e.g. Jacob and David, were sinners. At times they had disobeyed God, and they had been rebuked and punished for it. Lesser men were undoubtedly sinners too. Solomon admitted to the LORD, 'there is no man who does not sin' (1 Kings 8.46). Psalmists asked God not to judge men, for 'who could stand' (Pss. 130.3; 143.2). They thought that no one could. The wisdom writers said much the same sort of thing (Prov. 20.9; Eccles. 7.20). These writers all believed that sin is universal, and that no one had ever lived a life of perfect obedience.

There is a problem here: if God created human beings, how is it that they have all turned against Him? It is easy to understand that since people are given a free choice to obey or rebel, some have chosen to rebel. But it is difficult to understand why all people share together in sin. What drives us on to choose evil instead of serving the LORD? Is there some fault in human nature that makes us all behave in this way?

Many Christians look to Genesis 3 for an answer to this question. They say that the first man fell into sin, and passed on his fallen nature

'Human beings have freedom to choose between good and evil . . . each can respond
to God or turn away from Him. The human race has failed to make proper use of the
opportunities for living which God has provided' (pp. 74, 73). Poisonous fumes from
a smelting plant in Japan caused the death of many workers there, and turned
the valley into a desert where no trees or plants will grow. A little boy was severely
wounded and his parents killed when his home was shelled in a border 'incident' in
Palestine.

What sort of 'choices'—and whose—caused these evils? What other choices might
have prevented them?

to all his children. There is no doubt that this story deeply influenced the thinking of the Israelites. It comes from the earliest of the written records in Israel, and was probably among the earliest traditions. Yet even so, none of the later writers of the Old Testament used the story to help explain the universality of sin. It is difficult to tell whether any of them intended even to mention Adam by name, except in 1 Chronicles 1.1, since his name is one of the ordinary Hebrew words for *a man* (see Job 31.33 and the RSV footnote). Why were they so silent about this important matter?

There is another difficulty about this interpretation of the story of Adam and Eve. The story describes the experience of temptation, but it does not describe the tempter, except as 'the serpent'. Most Christians take this to be a name for Satan, but nowhere in the Old Testament is the serpent said to be Satan. The idea that the serpent was Satan, was first introduced in one of the books of the Apocrypha: Wisdom 2.24. In fact the serpent is described as directly opposed to God, and wanting to encourage evil. Yet in the rest of the Old Testament Satan is described as an angel whose work was simply to test the sincerity of those who served God. The two ideas could not be brought together until people had begun to think of Satan as having completely rejected the rule of God, and this idea was only developed after all the Old Testament books had been written.

3. THE PROBLEM OF EVIL

But even if we suppose that Genesis 3 was intended to describe the work of Satan, despite the fact that the Israelites did not relate the two ideas, there are still problems. If Satan is a fallen angel, as the New Testament suggests, we shall want to ask what caused him to fall. The blame for the origin of evil may perhaps be placed on this spiritual being instead of on man. But we still have no answer to the question: why did a creature made by God rebel? No real reason for Satan's choice of evil is given anywhere in the Bible. All that we can say about the origin of sin is that as soon as one of God's creatures sinned, he encouraged others to sin also. It is easier to suppose that the universality of sin results from the influence of one person on another, than from some inborn fault of character.

The value of Genesis 3 is not that it tells us of the historical origin of sin, but that it describes how evil gains a place in the lives of men in all ages, through the influence of one sinner upon another. We value this story highly because it describes experiences that we know only too well ourselves. The story describes the ways in which we are persuaded to disobey God.

(a) There is the suggestion that we do not know exactly what God wants us to do: 'Did God say?' (Gen. 3.1).

(b) There is the suggestion that God's commandments are unfair, and misleading (Gen. 3.4, 5).

(c) There is the suggestion that there is something to be gained by disobeying God: 'you will be like God, knowing good and evil' (Gen. 3.5).

(d) There is the encouragement to sin which comes simply from thinking about a disobedient act: it seems 'a delight' (Gen. 3.6).

(e) There is the encouragement to sin which comes because somebody else is willing to share our disobedience: 'She also gave some to her husband, and he ate' (Gen. 3.6).

In a later part of the story God challenged, first Adam, and then Eve, to explain their disobedience. Each in turn looked for somebody else to blame. They felt they had been persuaded to do evil. God recognized the power of persuasion, but he also recognized that each of them was free to refuse to be tempted. Each could have been obedient, and each deserved punishment for choosing to disobey.

The one new thing that came into the lives of both Adam and Eve because of their sin was their separation from God. They were driven out of the garden, and away from the intimate fellowship with the LORD described in the earlier part of the story. What they lost was 'knowledge of God' (see p. 66), and the grace to do His will that comes from fellowship with Him. If there is some inherited form of corruption which encourages men to disobey, it lies in this separation from God, which makes obedience impossible. The whole Bible is the story of God's work to bring man back into fellowship with Himself, and to establish a community of the righteous.

## STUDY SUGGESTIONS

WORDS

1. 'The Fall of Man': Which one of the following words best explains the meaning of 'fall' in that phrase?
   defeat   extinction   failure   retreat   ruin
2. 'The Lord repents of the evil' (pp. 73, 74).
   Which of the following alternatives best expresses the meaning of 'repents' in that sentence?
   (a) admits wrong-doing     (c) turns to a different way
   (b) asks pardon            (d) regrets previous action

CONTENT

3. (a) What explanation, if any, does Genesis 3 provide for the universality of sin?
   (b) If it provides none, what is the purpose of the story?
4. Why did the writers of the Old Testament not interpret the serpent in Genesis 3 as Satan?

BIBLE

5. (a) What evidence can you find in the Old Testament for the belief that evil-doers persuade others to do evil?

(b) How do the writers suggest that we avoid this influence?
Examine the phrases 'Come let us . . .', and 'Go not . . .', as they are used in the Old Testament writings.

6. (a) Examine the use of the word 'tempt' (or in RSV: 'test') in the Old Testament. Who most often is described as doing the tempting, and who is being tempted?

(b) How would you explain Deuteronomy 6.16?

DISCUSSION

7. (a) Why does God give people the freedom to choose how they will respond to Him?

(b) What difference would it make if people could only do good?

8. In what ways, if any, does belief in Satan help us to understand the nature of temptation, and in what ways does it hinder our understanding of temptation, and of the reasons why we fall into sin?

## SIN AND ITS RESULTS

I. SIN

Several different Hebrew words are used to express the general idea of sin. The meaning of each word varies, so that two such words can be used with identical meaning, or the same two words can be used to mean quite different things. This is a problem which all translators have to face, when trying to discover the exact meaning of what they are translating, and to express it accurately in the language of translation. And unless readers understand and can use the original language, they cannot be sure what words have been translated to give the words they read in their own languages. However, the translators of the Old Testament have tried to find the exact meaning of the Hebrew, and in the RSV, for example, they have tried to use the same English word wherever a similar meaning was intended. This is a help to those of us who cannot study the Old Testament in the original Hebrew.

There are two words which are used in the RSV to describe things done which are against the will of God. The first of these words is 'sin', which is a very general term and covers things done intentionally (Isa. 3.9; 30.1), as well as things done without intention to disobey (Lev. 4.13; Gen. 20.3–7). It may refer to something done against another man (1 Sam. 20.1), and it may also be used for something done against God Himself (Exod. 32.33).

The original meaning of the word to 'sin' was 'to miss the mark', or 'to miss the road'. It was used, for example, of an archer who failed to hit his target, or a traveller who lost his way. So now, when the word is used theologically, sin carries the meaning of 'failure': something that should have been done has not been achieved. A sinner is a person who has failed to do God's will, and has failed to live on good terms with his neighbour.

The second word is 'transgression'. It is used many times in the RSV to translate a Hebrew word which always means an intentional act against the will of God. A 'transgressor' is a man who *chooses* to disobey God, and who goes his own way without accepting the authority of God. The same Hebrew word which is often translated 'transgression' is also sometimes translated as 'rebellion', e.g. in 1 Kings 12.19. This was probably the original meaning of the Hebrew word. The same translation is used in Job 34.37, where Elihu describes Job by saying 'he adds rebellion to his sin'. Not only has Job failed to live as God wanted him to, he has deliberately *chosen* to disobey.

The attitude of mind which leads a man towards acts of sin or transgression is described by the word 'iniquity' (Job 31.24–28; Ps. 36.1–4). This fact helps us to understand Exodus 20.5 and similar verses: 'For I the Lord your God am a jealous God, visiting the iniquity of the fathers upon the children to the third and fourth generation of those who hate me'. The attitude of one person affects another, and the three or four generations (who could all be living at the same time) influence each other in their attitude to God. The father's iniquity is shared by his family, and all are guilty before God.

The people who are rebellious against God, and who refuse to do His will are frequently called the 'wicked' (Ps. 10.3). Such people are often set in contrast with the 'righteous', who do the will of the LORD (Gen. 18.23; Prov. 12.26). Job complains that both come to the same end in death (Job 9.22; compare Eccles. 9.2). The prophet Ezekiel recognized that a man might change from being wicked, and begin to live righteously (Ezek. 33.14–16), and that the righteous also could turn aside from God, and become wicked (Ezek. 33.13).

## 2. GUILT

A wicked person lives in a state of 'guilt'. He is liable to be punished for the evil he does. The prophets were deeply aware of the guilt of God's people, and continually warned them of punishment to come. They believed that the leaders of the nation were particularly guilty (Jer. 23.1–4). Among these were the kings (Hos. 5.1), prophets (Jer. 28.15, 16), priests (Isa. 28.7), and the richer and more powerful people generally (Amos 6.1).

But the prophets did not believe that the ordinary people had escaped being guilty (Hos. 4.12). Some of the Israelites supposed that they had escaped punishment, but the prophets warned them not to speak too soon (Jer. 5.12–15, compare Ps. 94.7). Hosea especially noticed their attitude, and warned the people that God was storing up judgement against them (Hos. 7.2; 13.12).

The writers of the Old Testament did not use a Hebrew word that could be translated 'conscience', but they were well aware of the feeling of guilt that is expressed by this English word. In the story of Adam and Eve we read that they hid themselves when God approached. Adam explained, 'I heard the sound of thee in the garden, and I was afraid, because I was naked; and I hid myself' (Gen. 3.10). When David had done wrong he felt guilty (1 Sam. 24.5; 2 Sam. 24.10). Isaiah felt distressed because he was 'a man of unclean lips' (Isa. 6.5). The compilers of Deuteronomy described the uneasy conscience that follows disobedience (Deut. 28.66, 67). A Psalmist described his own feelings of guilt before he repented (Ps. 32.3, 4). All these are accurate descriptions of an uneasy conscience. A sinner knows that he is guilty before God.

### 3. GOD'S WRATH

God's response to human guilt is 'wrath'. The nature of God's wrath is well described in Genesis 6.5–7; 'The LORD saw the wickedness of man ... and the LORD was sorry that he had made man on earth, and it grieved him to his heart'. The prophets spoke often of the wrath of God, e.g. Hosea 5.10; 13.11; Isaiah 9.19; 10.6; Jeremiah 7.29; 10.10; Ezekiel 21.31; 22.31; Zephaniah 1.18. Some of the Psalmists rejoiced that God's wrath would fall on evil-doers (Pss. 2.5; 21.9; 59.13). Others recognized that God's people deserved his wrath (Ps. 106.40–41). Some pleaded with God that he should not continue to show wrath towards them (Pss. 88.13–18; 89.46–48).

Many passages in the Old Testament describe how God restrains his wrath, and holds back the punishment that sinners deserve. The earliest traditions in the Torah, the J-traditions, include two promises which God made. The first, made after the flood, was that He would never again destroy in the same way (Gen. 8.21, 22). The second, given to Abraham, was that if there were ten righteous people in Sodom he would not destroy the city (Gen. 18.32). Moses pleaded with God not to destroy the Israelites after they had made the golden calf and worshipped it at Mount Sinai, and God restrained His wrath (Exod. 32.11–14). Amos was a prophet of judgement, yet we read that he also pleaded with God for Israel, and that God turned aside from carrying out His wrath (Amos 7.1–6). The significance of God's restraint is explained in the words of Ezekiel, 'As I live, says the LORD God, I have no pleasure in the death of the wicked, but that the wicked turn from his way and live' (Ezek. 33.11).

## 4. JUDGEMENT

God's wrath is not a blind fury, or an uncontrolled anger. It is aroused by sin (Deut. 7.4; Isa. 5.24–5). It leads on to judgement and punishment as the reasonable consequences of sin. From the earliest times God was recognized as 'the Judge of all the earth' (Gen. 18.25), but in the Torah 'judgement' was a responsibility given to men. There were rules about fair treatment of the accused. There was to be no injustice or partiality (Lev. 19.15). Judgements were to be based on God's ordinances (Num. 35.24).

The prophets recognized that the judges of their day were not giving judgement fairly, but were helping the rich and neglecting the poor (Amos 5.7, 12). The prophets believed that they themselves were sent to declare God's righteous judgements (Hos. 6.5; Mic. 3.8), but it is the LORD who judges His people (Isa. 3.14, 15; Jer. 1.16; Ezek. 5.6–8).

## 5. JUDGEMENT AND THE DAY OF THE LORD

God's judgement is often referred to as a future event, which will take place on 'the Day of the Lord'. But that 'Day' is not necessarily an event at the end of history. Many writers suggest that it is a moment in the course of history, a time that has since passed, so that we can look back and see that God did punish his people. For example it is suggested that the 'Day' which Amos predicted, actually came when the Assyrians conquered Israel, and destroyed the northern kingdom for ever (Amos 5.18–20). The 'Day' for Isaiah was the day when Judah would be punished for all her sins (Isa. 2.12–19). That day was postponed by God's purpose when the Assyrians failed to capture Jerusalem, but came when the Babylonians took her people into exile.

But these 'Days' did not bring a time of justice and peace on earth; men continued to live as transgressors, disobedient to God. So the Israelites were led to believe in another greater Day that was yet to come, when all evil-doers would be punished and righteousness would abound. This idea was expressed most fully in the apocalyptic writings of the Old Testament. See Isaiah 24—27, and Daniel.

## 6. PUNISHMENT

An important part of the teaching of the Old Testament about 'punishment' is that, in a world ruled by God, sin brings its own result, which is trouble. Solomon prayed at the dedication of the Temple that God would condemn 'the guilty by bringing his conduct upon his own head' (1 Kings 8.32). The same idea occurs in the Psalms (Pss. 9.16;

10.2; 141.10), and among the Proverbs (Prov. 5.22). God had revealed that the world had been created in such a way that it would help towards the fulfilment of His purposes. It could not easily be used to serve the purposes of the wicked. Their evil deeds could only cause trouble in such a world, and especially trouble for themselves.

Several writers ask why the wicked prosper (Ps. 73.3; Jer. 12.1). The answer given was that although they seemed to be secure (Job 12.6), they would be 'requited', i.e. paid back, for what they had done (Prov. 11.31; Ps. 28.3–5). 'What his hands have done shall be done to him' (Isa. 3.11). This is an example of what the Romans called the *Lex Talionis*: i.e. the belief that fair judgement involves a punishment equal to the crime. The earliest law code after the Ten Commandments includes the most famous statement of this rule. 'life for life, eye for eye, tooth for tooth' (Exod. 21.23–25). The prophets believed that God's own judgements were based on this rule (e.g. Hos. 4.6; Isa. 33.1, Jer. 30.16).

Because the people of Old Testament times had no clear idea of life after death, they believed that punishment of the wicked must take place in this life. It is even suggested in one place that death is an escape for the wicked (Job 11.20). All the disasters that fell on Job were thought to be the sort of thing that happened to the wicked: their possessions carried away (Job 20.28, 29), their children destroyed (Job 27.13, 14), their health ruined (Job 15.20). But the writer of Job described such popular beliefs in order to deny them. These same things happened to Job, even though 'there is none like him on earth, a blameless and upright man, who fears God and turns away from evil' (Job 1.8).

Many writers in the Old Testament describe the punishment of the wicked as the direct opposite of the blessings of the righteous, which were thought to be 'long life, many children, and their memory preserved in Israel' (p. 69). The LORD will not keep the wicked alive (Job 36.6; Prov. 10.27), they go down to Sheol (Pss. 9.17; 31.17), they will have no children (Job 18.19, compare Ps. 37.28, 38), their memory will perish, so that nobody will know their name (Job 18.17; Ps. 9.5; Prov. 10.7).

The writers seem to have felt strongly that God cannot endure the wicked. They have failed to reach the quality of life God planned for them, and are a hindrance to His purposes, so they must be got rid of (Ps. 37.10, 36; Prov. 10.25). They vanish (Ps. 37.20), destroyed by God (Gen. 18.23; 2 Sam. 4.11; Ps. 9.5). They are 'cut off' (1 Sam. 2.9; Ps. 37.28, 38), and perish (Ps. 68.2). But we need to remember that all these words could be used to describe physical death, since the Israelites believed that death brought the break-up of human nature. Only in Daniel 12.2 is there any idea of judgement and punishment after death.

'Because the people of Old Testament times had no clear idea of life after death, they believed that punishment of the wicked must take place in this life' (p. 82). The Egyptians, however, believed that the Pharaohs, and perhaps other royal leaders, could enter a new life after death. This papyrus shows the god Anubis weighing the soul of Hu-nefer to discover if he was worthy of life, and then introducing him to the god Osiris. To enter the underworld, it was believed, the king had to be innocent of evil, and reverent towards the gods.

83

## STUDY SUGGESTIONS

WORDS

1. (a) Use a dictionary to discover the various meanings of the two words 'present' and 'attend'. Then write two sentences using these two words in such a way that they have 'identical meanings', and two other sentences in which these words are 'used to mean quite different things' (p. 78).

   (b) Give examples of a similar kind that illustrate the difficulty of translating from English into your own language.

2. Which two of the following words could best be described as forms of 'iniquity' (see p. 79 for a definition of iniquity).

   bribery    murder    rebelliousness    theft    unkindness
   violence.

CONTENT

3. (a) What difference is there between a 'sin' and a 'transgression', as these words are used in the RSV to translate Hebrew words?

   (b) Express the thoughts contained in Isaiah 59.12, in your own words so as to show the differences between the three words used there for human evil.

4. What is the connection between human judgements and the judgement of God, according to the writers of the Old Testament?

BIBLE

5. (a) Discover what is said in the apocalyptic passages of Isaiah (chapters 24—27) about the 'Day of the LORD'.

   (b) How do these ideas differ from what is written about *that Day* in other parts of the Old Testament?

6. The word 'Hell' is often used in the New Testament to translate the Greek word *Gehenna* (see RSV footnotes). This name comes from the Hebrew for 'Valley of Hinnom'.

   (a) Find out and make notes on the information about the valley of Hinnom contained in the Old Testament.

   (b) What connection, if any, is there between the Valley of Hinnom and the New Testament ideas about Hell?

DISCUSSION

7. How would you answer a man who said, 'We are taught as Christians to be patient and forgiving, yet we often read in the Bible about the wrath of God.' Why is it right for God and wrong for us to be 'kindled to wrath'?

8. (a) What connection, if any, do you see between sin and death?
   (b) How do your ideas differ from those expressed in the Old Testament?
9. 'The writers of the Old Testament preach judgement, but the writers of the New Testament preach salvation.' Is this a fair assessment of the two parts of the Bible? Give reasons for your answer.
10. 'If the righteous is requited on earth, how much more the wicked and the sinner' (Prov. 11.31).
    (a) How would you explain this verse?
    (b) Do you agree with the view expressed?

# CHAPTER 5

# Salvation

## GOD'S ATTITUDE TO SINNERS

'The LORD saw that the wickedness of man was great in the earth, and that every imagination of the thoughts of his heart was only evil continually. And the LORD was sorry that he had made man on the earth, and it grieved him to his heart.'

(Genesis 6.5–6)

### I. THE NEED FOR A FRESH START

The editor of the J-traditions introduced the story of the flood with these words. They show that at a very early date in the history of Israel people began puzzling over the existence of evil in the thoughts and actions of mankind. God had created the world, and filled it with good things, and had given people the opportunity of enjoying these good things by serving Him. Yet they had chosen evil instead of good. They had acted against God's purposes, and had spoilt the world that He had made. What would God do about their disobedience? Why should He allow His creatures freedom to interfere with the fulfilment of His purposes?

The story of the flood suggests one answer that God might give to the problem. Genesis 6.7 describes God as saying, 'I will blot out man whom I have created from the face of the ground . . . I am sorry that I have made them.' The story goes on to tell how all the wicked were destroyed by drowning, and only Noah and his family survived. A later version of the story explains that 'Noah was a righteous man, blameless in his generation' (Gen. 6.9).

The story-tellers suggest that perhaps God was meaning to make a fresh start this way, with only the righteous to share his world. But before they came to the end of the account of the flood, they made it quite clear that this was not God's way of coping with the situation. We read that God said, 'I will never again curse the ground because of man, for the imagination of man's heart is evil from his youth' (Gen. 8.21). The account of the flood goes on to give details of the indecent behaviour of Noah and Ham, showing that even those who were supposed to be righteous did not live as God intended them to do (Gen. 9.21, 22).

All men richly deserved punishment and even death, because they had shared in spoiling the world God had created, and in rejecting the way of life He had offered to them. Yet God chose to save them from

86

the consequences of their sinfulness. There was nothing in their character or quality which could prompt Him to turn aside from punishing them: 'man's heart is evil from his youth' (Gen. 8.21). He could justly destroy them, but He would not. God's attitude to sinners does not depend on the rights and privileges of men; it derives from His own character and purposes.

The Israelites did not at first understand the ways of God, or know why He acted as He did. They gradually came to understand more as they experienced His activities among them. When the editor of the J-traditions commented on the story of the flood, he did not immediately point out the lesson it teaches about the character and purposes of God. Instead, he went on to tell of the experiences of the Patriarchs, and through these he gradually led his readers to a real awareness of all that God was doing in Israel.

## 2. GOD'S LOVE FOR HIS PEOPLE

Instead of destroying mankind, God chose one man through whom he would make Himself known. This man was Abraham. The relationship of Abraham and his descendants with God would show all mankind what God is like. This was the 'blessing' they would find (Gen. 12.3).

Later writers discussed God's motives in choosing the Israelites. He did not choose them because of their large numbers; they were not a powerful nation like the Egyptians or the Assyrians (Deut. 7.7). It was not because they were righteous that God favoured them; it was because other nations deserved to be punished (Deut. 9.4, 5). The real reason why God chose Israel was because he had loved their fathers (Deut. 4.37), and had continued to love their children (Deut. 7.9).

But what sort of love was it that God had for the people of Israel? The Hebrew word used for love in these verses, *Aheb*, was an ordinary word used for the feeling of one person for another: e.g. a man for his neighbour, a man for his wife, a parent for his child. Such love is often attracted by qualities in the person loved, but this is not always so. Hosea discovered that his love for his wife did not depend on her beauty, purity, or faithfulness. It continued even when she did everything she could that would make her repulsive to him. Through Hosea's own experience of love he was able to understand and describe something of God's feelings for Israel. It was in the nature of God to love mankind, and He showed that love in a special way in His relationship with Israel. The motive of God's loving activity in Israel is sometimes said to be 'for his own sake' (Isa. 48.11), or 'for his name's sake' (Ps. 106.8, Ezek. 20.9). These phrases simply mean that love is part of God's essential nature, and that He is true to His character in continuing to show His love for people even when they sin.

God's love for mankind always involves a desire to enter into a creative relationship with people. The various covenants which we shall study in the next section of this chapter all resulted from God's desire to establish fellowship with people. Often the people failed to fulfil the hopes expressed in the covenants, and continued in disobedience and sin. But God Himself never broke the covenants. He never withdrew from the relationships involved, so that whenever the people who had shared in the covenant returned to seek God's blessing, they always found Him ready and waiting to renew His relationship with them.

### 3. GOD'S FAITHFULNESS

This faithfulness of God to His purpose of love towards men is described in a special Hebrew word: *chesed*. Translators have always had difficulty in finding a suitable English equivalent for this Hebrew word. The RSV translators have used *steadfast love*, and this does seem to express the motive of God which led to the creation of the various covenants, and made their continuance possible even after men had failed to fulfil their part.

In Hebrew poetry the same ideas are often expressed twice over, using different words: e.g. 'Thou wilt show faithfulness to Jacob and steadfast love to Abraham' (Mic. 7.20). This 'parallelism', as it is called, helps us to understand the meaning of Hebrew words which might otherwise be difficult to translate. In this example 'steadfast love' is shown to be similar in meaning to 'faithfulness'. There are other examples of these two words being used in parallel, e.g. in Psalm 88.11. But other words also are used as similar in meaning to 'steadfast love'. Notice especially 'righteousness' in Hosea 10.12. This means that what is 'right' for God is that which supports and encourages the fulfilment of His purposes. Notice also 'compassion' in Lamentations 3.32.

Some writers group 'steadfast love' with other words which describe the character of God, and which show us what can be expected from Him. 'He is gracious and merciful, slow to anger and abounding in steadfast love' (Joel 2.13; compare Exod. 34.6). He is merciful (Isa. 63.7), and willing to forgive (Num. 14.19). His love is everlasting (Isa. 54.8; Ps. 100.5). All these words taken together provide us with a very accurate idea of the nature of God's 'steadfast love'.

It is not God's purpose to restrict His steadfast love to Israel. As early as the time of Amos it was recognized that He had shown His care to other nations (Amos 9.7). The Psalmists were confident that all men could depend on His goodness (Pss. 36.7; 145.9). The writers of the books of Jonah and Ruth deliberately set out to describe God's care for people who were not Jews (Jon. 4.10,11; Ruth 4.11–14).

All this evidence shows that God was revealing His steadfast love for mankind throughout Israel's history. He revealed Himself because of His love, and it was His love that He revealed.

## STUDY SUGGESTIONS

**WORDS**

1. 'And the LORD was sorry that he had made man on the earth, and it grieved him to his heart' (Gen. 6.6).
   Which two of the following words best describe the feelings implied in the statement that God was 'grieved to his heart'?
   anger   anxiety   disappointment   frustration   irritation
   resentment   pain
2. (a) Which three of the following words could be used instead of love in the expression 'steadfast love'?
   affection   admiration   appetite   devotion   need   sympathy
   (b) The three words you have chosen have slightly different meanings. Explain how each expresses something about God's attitude to men.

**CONTENT**

3. 'God's attitude to sinners does not depend on the rights and privileges of men; it derives from His own character and purposes' (p. 87). Explain in your own words what this means.
4. What difference in meaning is there, if any, between the two Hebrew words described in this section as meaning 'love', and 'steadfast love'?

**BIBLE**

5. (a) Use a Concordance to discover all the things that the Psalmists believed God would do 'for His own sake', or 'for His name's sake'.
   (b) What do these things suggest about the character of God as it was understood by the Psalmists?
6. The Hebrew word *chesed* is used several times by Hosea. See especially Hosea 4.1; 6.4–6; 10.12; 12.6. Can you suggest which of the English words in the RSV are used to stand for the word *chesed* in these verses? Who shows, or ought to show *chesed*, according to most of these verses?

**DISCUSSION**

7. (a) What is the meaning of the statement: 'for the imagination of man's heart is evil from his youth' (Gen. 8.21). In particular, what does the word 'man' mean here: (i) an individual, (ii) human beings in general, or (iii) the whole human race?
   (b) Which of the following is nearest in meaning to the statement?
     (i) 'Man' learnt evil while he was young and inexperienced, and ought not to be blamed for continuing in sin.

   (ii) 'Man' is thoroughly bad, not even in his youth did he do good. It is useless to hope for a change of heart, so God will leave him alone in his sin.
   (iii) 'Man' has no right to enter into fellowship with God, so God Himself must act by grace and forgiveness if man is ever to enjoy fellowship with Him.
8. 'True love needs no motive. It is spontaneous and enduring.' Is this true of human love, as well as of the love that God shows to men? Give examples.


## GOD'S WAY OF HELPING SINNERS

We have seen that the motive of all God's activities among men is love. In the beginning He created human beings to share a loving relationship with one another, and with Him. At the centre of all evil is lovelessness. Pride, greed, selfishness, and all the other forms of iniquity are denials of the way of love, and therefore are contrary to the will and purpose of God. People's lives have been spoilt by evil, so that they cease to give or receive love from one another. Human society has been spoilt because it is not built on the compassion and care which God intended to be at the centre of all human relationships. People are out of harmony with God, and at cross-purposes with Him.

But God continues to regard human beings with love. This love has the special qualities belonging to steadfastness. It is not caused by any attractiveness in man, but results simply from God's essential nature. It is God's will to re-create men so that they live the life of love which was His purpose in creation. It is His will to re-create human society so that all men can live in happy relationships with each other and with Him. This re-creation is what we call 'salvation'.

### I. THE COVENANTS

But how is this to be done? God chose to work for salvation by making covenants with men. A covenant is an agreement by which personal relationships are established. In human society marriage is a good example of a covenant. The relationship is based on love, but it is expressed through the marriage vows, and is fulfilled in married life. God's covenants are based on love. They are expressed in the terms of an agreement, and they are fulfilled in a creative relationship between God and men, and between men. The importance of these covenants is shown by the fact that the two parts of the Bible are known as the Old Testament and the New Testament. 'Testament' is simply another word for 'covenant'. The Bible is all about God's covenants with men.

When we study the Old Testament we discover that God made a whole series of covenants, not only one. He made covenants with Noah,

'People's lives have been spoilt by evil, but God continues to regard human beings with love. It is His will to re-create people so that they can live the life of love which was His purpose in creation' (p. 90).

Stretcher-bearers set out to rescue casualties from the flames after an air raid in Vietnam. Doctors and nurses in Malaysia prepare for an operation that will help a leprosy patient to lead a useful life again.

What is the difference, if any, between these 'rescues' and the 'salvation' which God offers to His people?

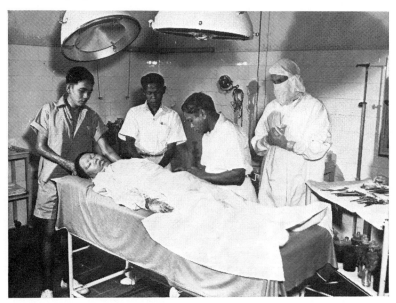

Abraham, the Israelites at Sinai, and with David. And the people themselves completed covenants with each other in the presence of God at Shechem and after the Exile in the time of Nehemiah. Jeremiah looked forward to a new covenant, which Christ established at the Lord's Supper.

Why were there so many different covenants?

It was not merely because men refused the relationship which God was offering them, and that the covenants were ended as a result. God could continue to offer that relationship so long as His love and mercy endured, i.e. for ever.

And it was not merely that God experimented with different sorts of covenant, hoping to find one which men would accept; that would suggest that God did not fully understand from the beginning what was necessary for man's salvation.

The real reason why there were so many covenants was that at each stage in the life of Israel God offered a relationship which people were capable of understanding, and accepting *at that time*. Each covenant expressed something more of God's purposes. Each one challenged the people to a deeper response and a fuller relationship with Him and with each other.

Sometimes those who introduced God's covenants to Israel could see further ahead, and could understand God's ways at a deeper level, than their fellows could. Moses, for example, seems to have expected that the people would respond more readily to the experiences at Sinai than they actually did (see Vol. 1, pp. 52–5). He seems to have expected that they would share his own experience of a direct relationship with God; but they refused and insisted that Moses should act as an intermediary between them and God (Exod. 20.18,19). God was concerned for the salvation of all the people, and provided for them a covenant which expressed the relationships that were possible for them all at that time.

Let us now look at each of the covenants in turn and the revelation of God that each contained:

(a) *The Covenant of Noah* (Genesis 9.8–17)

This passage comes from the P-traditions, but its ideas are in harmony with the promises of God in the J-traditions (see Gen. 8.20–22). This is the covenant between the Creator and His creatures. The very possibility of life is dependent upon God's maintaining the world that He created. By this covenant God promised that He would never again let loose the floods to destroy all living creatures. The rainbow was to be the sign of God's protective care. This covenant did not involve any conditions to control or direct the behaviour of mankind.

(b) *The Covenant of Abraham* (Genesis 15.7–21 and 17.1–27)

Here both the J- and the P-traditions give an account of the covenant which God made with Abraham. This was to establish the special role for which God chose the Israelites from among the nations. This covenant did not cancel the covenant with Noah, but prepared the way for an even greater blessing for mankind. It provided a basis for God's relationship with the family of Abraham. God would give them a land for their own use. He did expect obedience, but it was not to be based on any law-code. It was to be a personal response to God's will as He would make it known to men, through their relationship with Him. Circumcision was to be a sign to show who were the heirs of this covenant. Perhaps this was meant to be a personal sign of submission and obedience to God (see Vol. 1, pp. 35–6 for further information).

(c) *The Covenant with Israel at Sinai* (Exodus 19.3–8 and 24.3–8)
We have noticed the two different accounts which the book of Exodus contains, of the relationship between this covenant and the law-giving at Sinai (see Vol. 1, pp. 54–5). According to Exodus 19.3–8 the covenant was made before the law was given, according to Exodus 24.3–8 it followed on the giving of the Law.

Each of the two passages gives a quite different view of the significance of the Law, dependent on two different sets of traditions in Israel.

1. The first passage records that the people promised obedience before the Law was given, and the Law was added to help the Israelites understand what God required of them.

2. The second passage suggests that the Israelites were first given the Law, and then made a covenant to keep it.

The first of these accounts is in keeping with the earlier covenants. It shows that the relationship with God was founded on His love and goodwill. His people's obedience follows as an outcome of the relationship. The second account implies that the whole relationship with God was founded on obedience, and was totally dependent on the fulfilment of the Law. These two contrasting attitudes are to be found among the Israelites all through the remaining period of the Old Testament, and also at various times among Christians.

Why was the law introduced into the history of Israel at this particular time? It seems that until this time God had been making Himself known to individuals, and his covenants were based on personal relationships. But at Sinai God made Himself known to a larger group of people, who were gradually to be formed into a nation. There would always be some among the Israelites who could enjoy the same sort of personal relationship with God that the Patriarchs had enjoyed. Moses himself was one of these. But many of them were not yet ready for this sort of relationship with God, nor capable of showing obedience simply as a response to His love in that relationship. They were willing that their leaders should know God, but they wanted to keep at a safe distance from Him themselves. So God gave the Law to bridge the gap, and to enable them to know His will without being more personally involved. This is the significance of Exodus 20.18–20. God was willing to provide a covenant relationship in a form that people could readily respond to, but it still fell short of the personal relationship that God wanted with His people.

According to the P-traditions, the custom of observing the Sabbath was to be a sign of God's covenant at Sinai (Exod. 31.16). It was appropriate that a covenant involving all the people should be celebrated by a sign, such as the Sabbath, in which all could take part.

(d) *The Covenant at Shechem* (Joshua 24.14–28)
After the Israelites had settled in Palestine they understood that it was God who had given them the land. In their gratitude for this they were willing to make a vow of obedience to Him. Joshua warned them that they could not make any agreement with God that would compel Him to favour them (v. 19). God's love for His people had been freely given, and He was equally free to punish their evil-doing. This covenant too was founded on God's goodwill, and provided for a continuing relationship among the people themselves, and between the people and God. The tribes of Israel were only loosely linked at that time and the covenant helped to draw them closer together, and so to prepare them for full national life.

The Shechem covenant was important because the people themselves as a group took the initiative in response to God's goodness. The only sign required from them in return was that they should show their sincerity in promising to serve God alone, by ceasing to worship foreign gods.

(e) *The Covenant of David* (2 Sam. 7.8–17; 23.2–5; 1 Kings 8.22–26)
The different traditions which have been drawn together in the book of Samuel give conflicting evidence about the appointment of a king in Israel. Some passages suggest that this was an act of defiance against the LORD, but others suggest that God Himself initiated this new development in Israel's history.

By the time that David had established his rule as king, and had conquered Israel's enemies, the people were prepared to accept his reign as a gift from God. They believed that it was a fulfilment of God's purposes. Nathan expressed the belief that David's relationship with God was on the basis of a new covenant. He assured David that his family would continue to reign after him. Solomon accepted that his own reign was part of the fulfilment of this promise. The people of the Northern Kingdom rejected Rehoboam's claims to inherit these promises, but the people of the kingdom of Judah accepted the rule of the house of David throughout the years that led up to the exile.

After the exile the Jews looked eagerly for the Messiah who would inherit David's covenant, and so have authority to rule in the name of the LORD. In New Testament times the Jews found it difficult to believe that Jesus was the Messiah, because He had never ruled as king over the Jews. But the Christians believed that He had always had the right to rule, even in His life-time, and that after His death, resurrection, and ascension He came to rule eternally over all God's creation.

## 2. COVENANT RENEWALS

(2 Kings 23.1–3; Nehemiah 9.32—10.29)

The people of Israel often failed to fulfil God's purposes as described in the various codes of Law. Then their leaders would call them to turn back to the LORD and to serve him faithfully. These leaders recognized God's goodness in all his dealings with Israel, and believed that the people's disobedience had caused these times of national and personal distress. So it was logical to urge obedience, and to ask the people to commit themselves to the service of the LORD. Josiah did so after the discovery of the law book in the temple. Both Ezra and Nehemiah did so, though we find it difficult to be certain of the order of events in their time (see Vol. 2, pp. 136–9). But disobedience was a constant problem in Israel, and the prophets came to believe that God's people were incapable of changing their ways and serving the LORD (Jer. 2.22; 13.23).

## 3. THE NEW COVENANT

(Jeremiah 31.31–34; compare Jeremiah 32.37–41 and Ezekiel 36.24–28)

It was Jeremiah the prophet who recognized that man cannot change his own ways, and become righteous. He also recognized that God was preparing to do something new to enable men to serve Him! 'I will put my law within them, I will put it upon their hearts' (Jer. 31.33). Even though men failed to obey God, because of their sinfulness, God Himself would restore the relationship and make obedience possible.

What was the difference between Abraham, Moses, and others who had faithfully served the LORD, and the people of Israel who had failed again and again? It was a difference in the nature of their relationship with God.

The great leaders had entered into a living active relationship with God, and this had given them the inward resources to be obedient. But most of the Jews had only heard of the LORD at secondhand. They had been taught *about* him, but did not know Him in any personal way. So Jeremiah said: 'No longer shall each man teach his neighbour, each his brother, saying "Know the LORD, for they shall all know me from the least of them to the greatest, says the LORD"' (Jer. 31.34).

The personal relationship between God and man, expressed in the early covenants, was equally important in God's covenant with the nation and through them with all peoples. However, the work of God's self-revelation needed to be carried much further before the ordinary people would be ready for the blessings He had planned for them from the beginning. The coming of Christ was the completion of all that God had been doing in Old Testament times to make Himself known to men, and to offer to them that personal relationship which was at the centre of all His purposes. Ezekiel wrote, 'A new heart I will give you, and a new spirit I will put within you', and this promise was made available to all men through the work of Christ. The work of revelation leading to salvation was complete in Him. The New Covenant is totally adequate to meet the needs of mankind.

## STUDY SUGGESTIONS

WORDS

1. Which one of the following words best expresses the same idea as the word 'covenant' as described in this chapter?
   agreement    bargain    contract    guarantee    pact    promise
   ultimatum
2. Which one of the following ideas best expresses the meaning of 'relationship' as it is used in this chapter?
   (a) ancestry and kinship between people
   (b) association and behaviour between people
   (c) comparison and contrast between people

CONTENT

3. What is the meaning of the title of the two parts of an English Bible: the 'Old Testament' and the 'New Testament'? Does the New Testament *replace* the Old Testament? If not, suggest another verb to describe the relationship between the two.
4. Describe in your own words the two different traditions about the relationship between the Covenant and the Law at Sinai. Which of the two is nearest to the Christian attitude to the Law?

BIBLE

5. Not all covenants in the Old Testament are introduced and established by God.
   (a) What other covenants can you discover in the book of Genesis?
   (b) Are similar covenants known in the community in which you live? In what ways are they helpful to the life of your society?
6. Give evidence by chapter and verse for the fact that God's covenant with David was remembered throughout the periods for which there are written records of the prophets. (A Concordance will help you.)

DISCUSSION

7. 'God says that He loves you, but when you turn to Him you find that He only wants you if you will obey His laws.' Do you agree? Give reasons for your answer.

8. The Methodist Church invites its members to make a covenant with God, and to renew this covenant annually. What is your opinion of this custom? What are its advantages? What are any possible dangers?


# SACRIFICE

Many different forms of sacrifice are mentioned in the Old Testament, from the very earliest records right through to the latest writings. In Vol. 1 we noted some of the more important sacrificial customs, and the changes in practice, as they took place in Israel (see pp. 36, 62, 76, 144, 163). Here we need to consider what the sacrificial customs have to tell us about the Israelite understanding of God, and His relationship with His people.

## 1. SACRIFICE AND THE COVENANTS

The first thing we must remember is that Salvation depends on God, and not on man, so it is achieved through His Covenants, rather than through sacrifices. The ritual of sacrifice may be a way for the covenant people to approach God. But their relationship with God is established in the first place by a covenant, not by an act of sacrifice.

There are occasional references in the Old Testament to sacrifices by people of other tribes or nations, but they are based on the beliefs and customs of those people. The sacrifices which are significant for us are those made by God's chosen people. Some of the prophets looked forward to a time when all nations would come together to worship God, but they would do so by joining with the Jews, and receiving the benefits of God's covenant with them.

## 2. THE MOTIVES OF SACRIFICE IN ISRAEL

We have seen that, through His covenants, God drew the people of Israel into a relationship with Himself. The sacrifices enabled the people to express their relationship with God in three main ways:

(a) When the Israelites wished *to thank God* for His goodness to them as a nation and as individuals, sacrifices could express this thanksgiving; especially the thank-offerings (Lev. 7.12), and the burnt offerings (Lev. 1.10–13).

(b) When they wished *to share fellowship with God,* sacrifices in

'There are references in the Old Testament to sacrifices by people of other tribes or nations, but they are based on the beliefs and customs of those peoples' (p.97). These beliefs and customs are known to us partly from seals used at that time. Pictures were carved on these small cyclinders, which leave a rectangular impression when rolled on soft clay or wax. The Assyrian seal shown above, from about 1000 BC, portrays a worshipper making offferings to his god. The one below, from Syria about 85 BC, shows the god Ashur as a winged being at the top, pouring out his blessing on a prince (shown twice) standing beside a sacred tree and attended by another god.

which the worshippers ate part of the sacrificial animal provided for this need through a communal meal, for example the peace offering (Lev. 3.1–5).

(c) When the people were moved *to make atonement for their sins* both as individuals and as a nation, sacrifice gave ritual expression to their desire for healing of broken relationships, and went alongside confession and restitution, e.g. the sin offering (Lev. 4), the guilt offering (Lev. 5), and the annual Day of Atonement (Lev. 16). (See Vol. 1, p. 163.)

### 3. SACRIFICE AND OBEDIENCE

We must remember that the people using the sin offering and the guilt offerings were God's chosen people. They were already in a saving relationship with Him through the covenants. They knew the proper response to the love which God had shown through the covenants, i.e. obedience. Sacrifice could never be a substitute for obedience (1 Sam. 15.22; Ps. 51.17; Prov. 21.3). Several of the prophets spoke fiercely against the Israelites for supposing that God would be pleased with them because of the many sacrifices that they made. They made it quite clear to the Israelites that sacrifices were an inadequate response to God's love (Amos. 4.4, 5; 5.21–24; Isa. 1.10–17; Jer. 7.21–26). Sacrifices were simply an outward sign of the inward and personal response to God, which only fully showed itself in obedience to God's will and purposes.

### 4. DELIBERATE AND UNINTENTIONAL SIN

However, the People of Israel did not respond fully to all that God was doing among them. As a people and individually they still acted against God's purposes, even after they had accepted the covenants. If they deliberately disobeyed God, then they could no longer claim the privileges of the covenant relationship. People who refused to accept their responsibility to obey God were to be *cut off* (Gen. 17.14; Exod. 12.15; Lev. 18.29); they no longer counted as members of the covenant community. Jeremiah believed that the whole nation had rejected their relationship with God, and could only expect punishment (Jer. 7.28, 29). Sacrifices would not help those who were deliberately disobedient (1 Sam. 3.14; 15.24–26). They had sinned with a 'high hand' (Num. 15.30).

But not all the sins were the result of deliberate disobedience, even though they were against the will of God and hindered His purposes for mankind (see definition of *sin*, p. 79). The sacrifices for sin in Israel were only for sins of this kind, and they were a way by which people could renew their relationship of obedience by asking God's forgiveness.

## 5. CONFESSION AND RESTITUTION

The rituals of the sin offering and the guilt offering were only acceptable to God when they were accompanied by confession and restitution (Num. 5.7). The opposite attitude is described in Jeremiah 2.35, where the outcome is judgement.

Confession was an essential part of the personal guilt offering (Lev. 5.5, 6), and also of the national ceremony of the Day of Atonement (Lev. 16.21). Many of the Psalms express confession, and were no doubt used in temple worship, serving as part of the preparation for sacrifices (e.g. Pss. 32.5; 38.18; 41.4). Some of the Psalms reminded the worshippers that sacrifice alone was insufficient: what God really demanded was obedience (Ps. 40.6–8; 51.16, 17). No man could approach God and find blessing if he refused to admit his need for forgiveness, or if he intended to go on in sin.

But restitution also was necessary in order to remove the barrier to fellowship with God that sin had created. The guilt offering was a gift to God on account of 'a breach of faith', and 'unwitting sin' (Lev. 5.14–16). But if a man had injured a neighbour by his sin, then he must restore the relationship he had broken with his neighbour, before coming to bring a guilt offering to the LORD. (Lev. 6.1–7).

## 6. ATONEMENT

When a man had shared in a sacrifice with real sorrow for his past sins, and with a real intention to serve God, then the sacrifice made atonement for his sin. It removed the hindrance to a right relationship with God that the sin had caused. Scholars are not certain of the origin of the Hebrew word for atonement, but by comparison with related languages they suggest that it means either *to wipe away* (i.e. to remove the stain of sin), or more probably *to cover* (i.e. to ensure that the sin is no longer seen or remembered). Whichever is the more accurate interpretation, it is *God* who deals with the problem of sin. The sinner cannot claim any merit because of his confession, restitution, or offering to God through sacrifice. What he does by these actions is to return to a state in which he can benefit from God's loving concern for him.

## 7. THE 'SUBSTITUTIONARY' THEORY

Many present day preachers and some modern writers suppose that the main purpose of the sacrificial system in Israel was to provide a substitute to carry the guilt and bear the punishment due to the sinner. This is known as the 'substitutionary' theory of atonement. But the facts of the sacrificial system (e.g. as described in Leviticus 16) do not seem to support this interpretation. The only animal that was burdened with the sins of the people was the second goat in the ritual of the Day of Atonement, and this was not sacrificed but driven out into the wilderness (see Lev. 16.21, 22).

Most of the laws governing sacrifice laid emphasis on the purity and wholesomeness of the animal to be sacrificed (e.g. Lev. 22.17–25). The probable meaning of sacrifice is that by giving a valued possession to God, the worshipper was giving a sign of sincere intention to serve Him. The life of the animal given in sacrifice was symbolic of the human life being given up to the service of the LORD (Lev. 17.11; Deut. 12.23). The gift was significant when it expressed the love and devotion of the giver.

## 8. ISAIAH 53

This important chapter needs a special comment. The interpretation we give to sacrifice will affect our understanding of it, and especially of Isaiah 53.5. Those who accept the substitutionary theory of the Atonement will interpret this verse as meaning that God poured out on His Servant the wrath that was due to human sin. They will say that there can be no forgiveness until just punishment has been exercised, and that the Servant took that punishment on himself in order that human beings might be forgiven.

But that interpretation is in direct conflict with the belief that God's motive in all his dealings with men has been steadfast love and mercy. God is ready to forgive long before man is ready to respond to His love. His covenants are offered long before man is committed to obedience. Sacrifice expresses man's response, not God's act of salvation.

So it seems right to interpret Isaiah 53 in a different way, which reflects all that we have discovered about God from our study of Old Testament Theology. As we saw in studying the Servant Songs (Vol. 2, pp. 57–58), 'the Servant stands for any among the Jews who were faithful to God'. Such people were very few; most of the Jews were rebellious and sinful. Those who were faithful shared the sufferings of those who were justly punished by being sent into Exile. They could have resented that suffering, and could have shown their resentment by rebelling against God like the others. But God was preparing to use them to bring renewal to Israel. By their example He would keep His purposes before the minds of the whole people. By their faithfulness He would eventually establish a new community who would serve Him. Only as they accepted a share in the suffering of Israel, and yet remained faithful, could God use them to bring salvation to the whole people. If they failed, the only alternative would be the complete rejection of Israel. By their patience and faithfulness new life would come to God's people.

Christ's suffering on the cross has always been interpreted in the light of Isaiah 53, and if we understand that chapter correctly we shall

SALVATION

appreciate what He achieved. He was the one faithful Israelite among the many who sinned, and their failure and rebellion was the direct cause of His suffering. This was so, not because God was punishing Christ for what the Israelites had done. It was so because He shared the life of God's people on earth, with all the pain of the strained relationship resulting from their disobedience. He never turned away from all that was involved in serving God among sinful men, even when it led to the cross. And so He provided the basis of a community of those who would serve God, and accept his leadership. His life given to God was the perfect sacrifice, expressing the complete obedience which the sin offerings and guilt offerings symbolized.

## STUDY SUGGESTIONS

**WORDS**

1. Which two of the following words best express the purpose of sacrifice in the Old Testament?
   compensation    dedication    destruction    loss    obedience
   punishment
2. The following words are all used in this chapter:
   (a) atonement    (b) confession    (c) forgiveness    (d) restitution
   (e) substitution
   Which of the definitions below belong to each of these words?
   (i) 'showing steadfast love and mercy'
   (ii) 'taking the place of, suffering instead of'
   (iii) 'admitting and regretting wrong-doing'
   (iv) 'removing the hindrance to a right relationship'
   (v) 'putting right an injury done to somebody'

**CONTENT**

3. 'The sacrifices enabled the people to express their relationship with God' (p. 97). What were the three qualities of that relationship which could be expressed by means of sacrifices?
4. (a) Why did the prophets criticize sacrificial worship so sharply?
   (b) Why did sacrifices nevertheless remain important in Israel?

**BIBLE**

5. Read the account of the Festival of the Day of Atonement in Leviticus 16, and answer the following questions:
   (a) For what individuals and groups is Atonement made in this ceremony?
   (b) In what way do you think 'the holy place and the tent of meeting and the altar' needed atoning for? (see v. 20).

(c) Which of the animals used in the ceremony were considered to be sin offerings or guilt offerings? Which of them is *not* described in this way?

(d) What was done with the blood of the bull and the goat which were sacrificed? What do you think was the meaning of this action?

(e) What was done with the goat over which all iniquities, transgressions, and sins of the people were confessed?

6. Which of the covenants which the LORD made with his people were associated with an act of sacrifice, and what significance had the sacrifice in the establishment of the covenant?

DISCUSSION

7. Does the LORD's Supper have a similar significance for Christians as the sin offerings and the guilt offerings of Old Testament times had for the Israelites? Explain the similarities and the differences.

8. 'It was the will of the LORD to bruise him; he has put him to grief' (Isa. 53.10).

Say how you think this statement applies to:

(a) the righteous in Israel at the time of the Exile,

(b) our LORD Jesus Christ.

9. Compare the Israelite idea of the purpose of sacrifice, as described in this chapter, with the purpose of any act of sacrifice that has had a traditional place in the life of your country, or people. Explain ways in which they are similar, or different from each other.

# CHAPTER 6

# The New Life

Two questions arise from all that we have studied so far:
1. What is the present outcome of God's work of salvation?
2. What will be the final outcome?
These are the subjects of this chapter and the next. First we must think about the results of God's work among His people in the times described in the Old Testament. These results are relevant for us today because God continues His work of salvation among us.

## THE 'REMNANT'

In the old Testament the people who would respond to the steadfast love of God, and who would try to live life as God intended it to be for them, are often described as the 'Remnant'. They would be very few in number. Most of the prophets looked forward to this Remnant as though they would be the ones saved at a later date, when God's punishment had already fallen on Israel. But they connected the experience of God's judgement with the historical events of their time, and they believed the Remnant would come at the moment in history when His judgement was carried out, i.e. close to their own time.

Amos, Micah, and Isaiah of Jerusalem made most use of the idea of the Remnant. They lived in a time of national disaster, when the northern kingdom was being destroyed by Assyria, and the southern kingdom of Judah was being defeated. These prophets believed that after that time a few people would remain who had been saved from destruction by God's mercy, and these people would serve the LORD (Isa. 10.20; Mic. 4.7; Amos 5.15). What the prophets seem not to have foreseen, was that, even among the Remnant who were actually saved from destruction, there would be many who failed to respond to God's steadfast love, and did not live as God intended them to do. Throughout the history of Israel there would be a conflict between the faithful and the unfaithful, between the righteous and the wicked.

Jeremiah realized that the Israelites who escaped the exile could not be relied upon to appreciate what God had done among them. Therefore he regarded the Remnant in Judah as of no use to God (Jer. 24.8–10). Instead, Jeremiah put his hope in the people taken into exile (Jer. 24.4–7). He believed that after their time of punishment they would return to serve the LORD.

Zephaniah, who worked at about the same time, did not share Jeremiah's despair about the people who remained in Judah (Zeph. 2.7; 3.12, 13). But the history of that period shows that Jeremiah was right, even though far fewer of those who returned from exile responded to God, than could have been expected. Throughout the history of Israel the faithful Remnant were always a small minority among those who survived the national disasters. Though many of the writers of the Old Testament clearly believed that God's work of salvation might be completed in their own time, they came to realize that the 'saved' in Israel, i.e. those who served the LORD, would always be few compared with those who disobeyed Him. The Remnant must live their life of obedience among many who would not serve the LORD.

Since God's purpose is to create a community of men and women who serve Him gladly, and live in peace and harmony with each other, His work of salvation is directed to that purpose. Throughout history He has been drawing people into fellowship with Himself, and with each other. Such fellowship has been possible wherever people were willing to respond to His steadfast love. Let us now examine what the Old Testament writers had to say about these relationships.

## OUR RELATIONSHIP WITH GOD

Three ideas are used in the Old Testament to describe the relationship between responsive men and the loving God: fear, faith, and love.

### I. THE FEAR OF GOD

Christians often describe their religion by saying, 'I believe in the Lord Jesus Christ.' The Jews expressed their religious experience by saying, 'I fear God' (Gen. 42.18; Exod. 18.21), or 'I fear the LORD' (2 Kings 4.1; Isa. 11.3). This way of expressing their relationship with God probably resulted from the Israelites' deep sense of God's *holiness*. The Hebrew word used for 'holy' probably meant 'separate'. Thus God's holiness is all that makes Him different from human beings, everything that makes Him seem mysterious and strange. There is an English word, 'awe', which sums up the human response to the holiness of God. It includes both wonder and dread; a desire to know, and also a fear of finding out, what God is like (see Gen. 28.17; Exod. 15.11).

The whole evidence of Old Testament revelation is that this holy God intends human beings to know Him. Hosea expressed this in the words of God;

> I am God and not man,
> the Holy One in your midst,
> and I will not come to destroy.
> (Hos. 11.9; compare Ezek. 39.7)

Isaiah of Jerusalem and Deutero-Isaiah shared this idea, and referred to God as 'the Holy One of Israel'. This suggests that God is different from men, but seeks relationship with them (Isa. 1.4; 41.14). For human beings, fear remains a real part of their experience of God's presence, even though God's purpose in making Himself known is for their good (Isa. 41.14; 54.4, 5).

Rightly understood, God's holiness leads to joy, as men share in His good purposes for them (Isa. 41.16, compare 48.17). This fear and this joy do not conflict, since it is the fear of the LORD which turns men from evil, so that they may share in good (Prov. 3.7; 8.13). Then they see the Law as a guide, showing them how to reverence God (Deut. 17.19; 31.13). The fear of the LORD leads men to walk in His ways (Deut. 10.12; Jos. 24.14; Ps. 86.11). It is the true basis of all wisdom (Prov. 9.10).

## 2. FAITH IN GOD

God's own *faithfulness* is frequently mentioned throughout the Old Testament (e.g. Deut. 32.4; Isa. 49.7; Ps. 89.8). God can be trusted, because He is always the same. His attitude to men is always one of *steadfast love*. The two ideas are nearly always linked, in Old Testament thought. In many of the Psalms faithfulness and steadfast love are set in parallel to each other (e.g. Pss. 36.5; 88.11). In prose passages also, the two ideas are often set side by side (e.g. Exod. 34.6; 2 Sam. 2.6; Hos. 2.19, 20).

In the Old Testament, God's faithfulness is often linked also with His *righteousness* (Ps. 85.11; Zech. 8.8). We have seen that 'righteousness' meant 'that which is according to God's will' (see p. 34). So God's righteousness is shown by the fact that He acts according to His purposes. The fact that He always does so is a measure of His faithfulness.

Another related idea is that God is a God of *truth* (Isa. 65.16; Jer. 10.10). In Hebrew the words for 'truth' and for 'faithfulness' come from the same verbal root. But the connection in thought is even more important than the relationship of the word forms. Truth is something which brings understanding, and provides meaning and purpose for life. For example, if it is true that God loves me, this is so wonderful that it must affect my whole life. Or again, if it is true that I am a sinner, then I must search out the way of salvation and find God's forgiveness. Truth is vitally important to me, and to us all. According to the Old Testament writers, God is a reliable source of truth. That is part of the meaning of the word 'faithful' when it is used about God. He can be trusted to give us a proper understanding of life and of ourselves.

Some of the Psalmists looked to God for truth (Pss. 25.5; 43.3). Psalm 119, the great Psalm in praise of the Law, teaches that the Law is true (vv. 142, 151). The Law is a source of the knowledge and understanding which gives us a sure foundation for life. Some of the books contained in the third section of the Hebrew Scriptures were written in order to preserve and pass on truth (Prov. 22.20, 21; Eccles. 12.10; Dan. 11.2).

The human response to God's revelation of His faithfulness and His truth should be faith. There are several examples in the Old Testament, e.g.

(a) Abraham 'believed the LORD, and the LORD reckoned it to him as righteousness' (Gen. 15.6). By his faith Abraham entered into a right relationship with God; he was responsive to God's purposes, and so he was righteous.

(b) Isaiah urged Ahaz to place his trust in God, by saying, 'If you will not believe, surely you will not be established' (Isa. 7.9). Unless Ahaz responded in faith to God he could not share in God's purposes, and his reign as king of Judah would be short and ineffective.

(c) Habakkuk believed that God's purposes would be fulfilled, and that those who opposed God would fail; 'but the righteous shall live by his faith', i.e. he would share in God's rule because he had faith (Hab. 2.4).

Faithfulness was clearly an essential part of serving the LORD. Ezra recalled Abraham's faithfulness with approval (Neh. 9.7, 8). A man of God delivered a message from God to Eli; 'I will raise up a faithful priest, who shall do according to what is in my heart and in my mind' (1 Sam. 2.35). David was described as more faithful than any other of Saul's household (1 Sam. 22.14). The descendant of David who would rule in God's name would be clothed in faithfulness (Isa. 11.5; compare Isa. 16.5). God's 'servants', i.e. those in Israel who would serve Him, would be faithful (Isa. 42.3).

In some of the verses we have quoted, faithfulness seems to mean 'trustworthiness', rather than 'trustfulness'. But we must remember that a person becomes trustworthy through being trustful towards God. The security which we discover through our relationship with God, enables us to be secure in our dealing with others (1 Kings 2.4; 3.6; and compare Ps. 26.3). Notice how the Psalmists use such words as 'fortress', 'rock', 'refuge', to describe the security they find in God, and the confidence He gives them for life (Pss. 18.2; 91.2; 144.2).

## 3. LOVE FOR GOD

The qualities of the right human response to God are the result of God's relationship with human beings. Because God is holy, we rightly respond by fearing Him. Because God is faithful, we can rely upon Him and have faith in Him. But we have already discovered that the most important thing about God's relationship with us is His love. We saw that God's love is described by two different words in the Hebrew

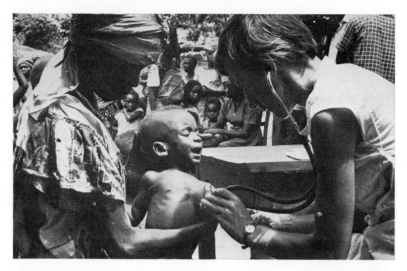

'The human response to God's revelation of His faithfulness and His truth should be faith' (p. 107).

West African mothers bring their babies for treatment because they themselves have experienced the nurse's skill and care. Voters in East Africa support the politicians who have shown honesty and concern for the people's welfare.

Give some examples of the ways in which human beings show their faith in God's faithfulness.

of the Old Testament (see p. 87). One is the ordinary word used for love between human beings. The other includes the idea of faithfulness, as shown by God towards men. In the RSV it is usually translated 'steadfast love' (see p. 88).

How did the writers of the Old Testament describe man's response to God's love? Did they think that human beings could love God as He loves them? They rarely use the word normally translated 'steadfast love' to describe the human response to God.

(a) *Hosea* taught the people of his time that God desired steadfast love, and he set this quality alongside 'knowledge of God' (Hos. 6.6). He also complained that, 'There is no faithfulness or kindness, and no knowledge of God in the land' (Hos. 4.1). In this verse Hosea was probably trying to describe what man's response to God ought to be, rather than what the relationship between human beings should be. He used the Hebrew word for steadfast love, although in this case it has been translated 'kindness' in the RSV.

(b) *Jeremiah* believed that in the early period of God's relations with Israel, men had shown steadfast love *to God*. In the RSV Jeremiah 2.2 is translated: 'I remember the devotion of your youth', but the word 'devotion' translates the Hebrew word normally translated 'steadfast love'.

(c) Similarly, in *Jonah* 2.8 the same word is translated 'true loyalty'. Here again the complaint is that this quality is lacking from the relationship of men with God.

The evidence of the whole history of Israel is that the Jews did *not* respond to God with steadfast love, so it is not surprising that this quality is not named in describing the existing relationships between men and God.

The ordinary Hebrew word for love is widely used in the Torah. Jesus quoted Deuteronomy 6.5 as one of the two commandments on which all the law and the prophets depend (Matt. 22.40): 'You shall love the LORD your God, with all your heart, and with all your soul, and with all your might.' The word 'love' here translates the Hebrew word which is normal for human relationships, e.g. for a man's relationship with his wife, a father's with his son. The same Hebrew word is used in the Ten Commandments, in referring to the thousands of 'those who *love* me [i.e. who love God] and keep my commandments' (Exod. 20.6; Deut. 5.10). The same word is used throughout the book of Deuteronomy to describe man's proper attitude to God.

So we can say that in the Old Testament both Hebrew words for love are used to describe how human beings *ought* to feel towards God, rather than how they do in fact feel and believe. Both the complaints of the prophets and the instructions of the law-givers guide men towards the unfamiliar path of love towards God.

Yet there is also evidence in the Old Testament to show that some of the people did respond to God's love. We find this evidence in the frequent use of words expressing thanksgiving and joy.

The Hebrew word for *thanksgiving* appears again and again in the Psalms. One verse in particular is often repeated:

'O give thanks to the LORD, for he is good,
for his steadfast love endures for ever' (e.g. Ps. 136.1).

This verse expressed thanksgiving which is basically a response to God's steadfast love. Sometimes the Hebrew word for thanksgiving is translated as *praise*. But 'praise' is more often used in the RSV to translate another Hebrew word, which elsewhere is translated as *Hallelujah*, meaning 'Praise the LORD'. (See for example Psalm 150. Notice also the 'Hallelujah' Psalms mentioned in Vol. 2, p. 100.)

Several different Hebrew words express the idea of *joy*, or *rejoicing*. For example they express the feelings of satisfaction which people have when a purpose is fulfilled or a task completed (Isa. 9.3). The wicked are said to 'rejoice' in the evil they have done (Ezek. 36.5; Prov. 2.14). The righteous 'rejoice' in what God has done: they rejoice in His salvation (Ps. 51.12; Isa. 12.3), His judgements (Ps. 97.8), and His deliverance (Ps. 9.14). Some of these verses express joy in what God has done for individuals, others express joy in what he has done for the whole people. Joy is especially related to the good fortunes of Jerusalem. Joy disappears when that city is defeated, and reappears when its future seems good (Isa. 51.11; Jer. 31.13). Joy is the people's proper response to God's steadfast love (Ps. 31.7). Because all God's purposes are good, and His achievements are sure, it became natural for the Old Testament writers to speak of having joy, or rejoicing *in the LORD* (Isa. 29.19; 41.16).

## STUDY SUGGESTIONS

WORDS

1. Which *two* of the following words come nearest to expressing what the Old Testament writers meant by the 'fear' of the LORD?
   anxiety    apprehension    horror    mistrust    panic    respect
   reverence    suspicion
2. An act of 'trusting' has happy results if the person concerned is 'trustworthy'. What quality is required in a person for each of the following sorts of action to have happy results?
   believing    depending    having faith    loving    relying
3. 'Hallelujah' transliterates a Hebrew phrase meaning 'Praise the LORD'.

(a) Describe in your own words what is meant by 'transliteration' (if necessary use a dictionary to help you).

(b) If you can, give some examples of transliteration, either into English or into any other language you know.

CONTENT

4. 'The qualities of the right human response to God are the result of God's relationship with human beings' (p. 107). Give three examples of God's relationship with human beings, and the human response that is appropriate as a result.

5. How are God's faithfulness, His righteousness, and His steadfast love related to each other?

BIBLE

6. Give a brief explanation of each of the following verses:
   (a) Ps. 119.142    (b) Isa. 7.9    (c) Isa. 16.5

7. Is it true to say that Old Testament writers never describe humans as showing steadfast love? Use a Concordance to check the answer to this question. In what context, if any, do humans show steadfast love?

DISCUSSION

8. 'The prophets were always too pessimistic about the response of men to the steadfast love of God. In fact there was a greater response than they imagined.' Do you agree with this statement? Give reasons for your answer, and illustrate it by quotations from some of the prophets about the Remnant.

9. 'The study of Old Testament Theology depends upon a knowledge of the languages used by those who wrote the Old Testament.' Do you agree with this statement? What difficulties arise because most people have to use Bibles in which the Hebrew and Aramaic are translated into other languages?

## OUR RELATIONSHIP WITH EACH OTHER

Whenever God called someone to serve Him, He did so in order that that person might have an influence within the community in which he lived.

God called Abraham to establish a family that would serve Him. He called Moses to draw the tribes of Israel together to become the People of Israel. He called David to establish the nation of Israel, freed from their enemies and able to serve the LORD.

But it was not only the great leaders whom God intended to have an influence in Israel. Every person who was responsive to the steadfast

111

love of God, was to set an example to the people of his day. His life was ruled by God, and this should have an effect upon his relationship with his fellow men.

The Law, the Prophets, and the Writings all contain guidance about how the people ought to behave as members of the Israelite community. All the codes of Law (described in Vol. 2, pp. 20–23) contain rules of conduct intended to establish good human relationships in Israel. A great part of the message of the prophets was a warning about the sins which were dividing the people and hindering God's purposes for them. The writers of the Wisdom literature, e.g. Proverbs, preserved an understanding of life which was drawn from practical experience, and which showed the best ways to live in God's world, and among His people.

We cannot in this Guide study all these parts of the Bible in detail. Ethics are a separate subject from theology, whether we are studying the teachings of the Old Testament or modern theory and practice. But it is important for us to recognize the reasons behind the rules for moral behaviour in Israel.

Throughout the Old Testament, ethics, i.e. the accepted customs, are not merely ways of behaviour which ease the problems that arise in human society, and help people to avoid conflict. As we have seen, righteousness is that which is in harmony with the will and purpose of God. All the law-giving, preaching, and teaching recorded in the Old Testament is intended to help people understand what it is that God wants them to do, and how they may best serve Him.

We shall see this clearly if we study the ethical rules contained in the Ten Commandments. These were the basis for many of the ideas about moral problems which are contained in other parts of the Old Testament. They show just what is involved in serving God in this world, and thus what sort of character people develop through obedience to the Law. We shall see that this can be summed up in the phrase 'the image of God' (see Gen. 1.26).

I. THE TEN COMMANDMENTS

In Volume 1 of this course (pp. 57–61) we examined the first four commandments, which concern relationships between men and God, and also noted the very special relationship between a man and his parents which is implied in the fifth commandment. It will be useful at this point to read through those pages again. But we must now look more closely at the final five commandments, which are the basis for all human relationships in the purposes of God (see Exod. 20.13 -17, Deut. 5.17–21).

*You shall not kill:* Respect for human life is central to Old Testament morality. It results from the knowledge that human life is a gift from God, and must not be carelessly or violently destroyed. The later

'All the law-giving, preaching, and teaching recorded in the Old Testament is intended to help people understand what it is that God wants them to do, and how they may best serve Him (p. 112).

In the eighteenth century BC Hammurabi, king of Babylon, had this stele set up in his kingdom. The carving at the top shows the sun god, Shamash, giving Hammurabi a sceptre and ring, the symbols of authority. The inscription below gives laws for the guidance of community life (but it does not say that these were revealed by Shamash).

There are similarities between the code of Hammurabi and the law codes of the Old Testament, but also many differences. There is no evidence that Moses and the later law-givers borrowed ideas directly from Hammurabi's code, and it is doubtful whether all the peoples ruled by Hammurabi adopted his code as a guide for daily life. Here is a passage from Hammurabi's code:

'If a citizen has destroyed the eye of one of citizen status, they shall destroy his eye. If he has broken the bone of a citizen, his bone shall they break.

If he has destroyed the eye, or has broken the bone, of a vassal, he shall pay one mina of silver.'

What similarities and what differences do you notice between this passage and the laws recorded in Exodus 21.2–35; Leviticus 24.17–20, and Deuteronomy 19.21?

codes of law distinguish killing which is blameworthy, from killing which is accidental (e.g. Exod. 21.12–14), or a just punishment for evil (e.g. Exod. 21.15–17). God offers every man the opportunity of responding to Him and sharing in His purposes. Since the Old Testament writers did not believe in an after life, they believed that death prevents a man from sharing in these blessings. Anyone who deliberately robbed another of the opportunity to serve God, by killing him, was deserving of death himself. And anyone who deliberately and openly defied God, or acted against His purposes, was considered equally deserving of death.

*You shall not commit adultery:* According to the stories of creation, sexuality is a gift from God, and normal relations between a man and his wife were encouraged and approved. God had said 'Be fruitful and multiply' (Gen. 1.28; compare Gen. 2.24). Serious misuses of sex were condemned in the later law codes e.g. sexual relations outside marriage (Exod. 22.16), prostitution (Lev. 19.29), homosexual relations (Lev. 18.22), and most especially adultery (Lev. 20.10). These actions are wrong because they are contrary to the purposes of God, and because they cause great misery and destroy trust.

Polygamy was not condemned, nor was the possession of concubines. Both could result in fairly permanent relationships, and children born from them would be well cared for. Yet towards the end of Old Testament times these customs were very rarely practised. No doubt the Israelites considered them to be less than the best sorts of relationship, but even the latest of the law-givers did not condemn them. This was probably because so many of the leading Israelites of earlier times had followed these customs, and the Jews would not have accepted open condemnation of them.

Divorce was only permitted in Israel when the marriage relationship was considered improper, e.g. because the woman was not a virgin at the time of marriage (Deut. 22.13–21), or because a man had married a foreigner (Deut. 7.3; Ezra 10.10, 11).

Several of the prophets accused the Israelites of committing 'adultery' by deserting the LORD in order to serve false gods (e.g. Hos. 2.7; Jer. 3.9. Ezek. 16.32). They expressed great horror at what God's people had done, and thus showed how highly they valued the marriage relationship. They felt it was right to compare the relationship between God and His people with that between a man and his wife.

*You shall not steal:* God's purpose is that all men should have sufficient of the good things of this world to enable them to live productive and healthy lives. When a person steals, he is trying to gain more than his fair share of these good things, by depriving somebody else of their share. This is made clear by the wide range of behaviour which the later law codes condemned as being forms of theft. These include dishonesty in trade (Lev. 19.35, 36), in employment (Lev. 19.13), in the exercise of a trust (Exod. 22.7-9), and in control of property (Deut. 19.14: the word 'landmark' means a boundary stone).

The wrong done by destroying property belonging to somebody else (e.g. by trespass, or by arson) is another closely related idea (Exod. 22.5, 6). Anyone who breaks these laws does not benefit himself, but robs another of his possessions.

We may wonder what was meant by the ban on charging interest on a loan (Lev. 25.35-38). This did not refer to ordinary commerce, where it is fair that those who provide money for a business should share in the profits. It applies to professional money-lenders who take advantage of people who are reduced to poverty and need financial or other help for a time until they can earn enough to pay for what they need.

*You shall not bear false witness against your neighbour:* God's purpose is that each person should have a place in human society, and good relationships with his fellows. Good relationships are destroyed when one person tells lies about another, so lies spread through conversation are condemned: this is slander (Lev. 19.16). And lies told by a witness in a law court are also condemned (Exod. 23.1-3, 6-9). A man must not lie for the sake of a bribe, but neither must he lie to protect somebody who is poor. His lies will prevent justice being done, and somebody will suffer who does not deserve to do so.

Notice that the commandment to 'love your neighbour as yourself' comes in a passage which condemns false witness (Lev. 19.15-18). Everyone with whom a man has to do, should be treated fairly, for only in that way can a strong human community be established. Desiring vengeance or bearing a grudge are as bad as actually spreading lies. All these attitudes are the opposite of love, and will destroy human relationships.

*You shall not covet ... anything that is your neighbour's:* This commandment is close in meaning to the eighth commandment: you shall not steal. To 'covet' means 'to have a strong desire to possess' (Deut. 7.25). To steal means actually taking something which belongs to someone else (Mic. 2.2). But even when a person restrains his covetousness, so that he does not actually steal something, his desire to possess it can have a strong effect upon his relationships with other people. Covetousness destroys friendships more quickly than anything else can. It is wrong in the sight of God because it destroys that human fellowship which is part of God's purpose in creation (Prov. 21.26).

Sometimes people suggest that the tenth commandment is more important than the others we have studied here, because it is about feelings and intentions, while the other four are about outward actions. But all such actions result from feelings and intentions, and the inward attitudes become important when they result in action. Sin is both feelings and intentions, and the resulting actions that are contrary to the purposes of the LORD. Paul suggests that knowledge of God's purposes as revealed by the law prompts men to further sin. There is a rebelliousness in human beings which makes them act deliberately against the will of God, just as a child is prompted to disobey his father's rules, simply because he knows they *are* rules (Rom. 7.7–12).

## 2. THE IMAGE OF GOD

According to Genesis 1.27, man was created in the image of God. We have seen that this probably did not mean that God and men share a physical likeness, but rather that they are both spiritual beings. The finest qualities possible in human life are a reflection of the character of God Himself. If God is holy, and faithful, and shows steadfast love, then those who serve Him must show similar characteristics in their relationships with their fellow men.

(a) *Human Holiness:* Holiness is probably the most difficult quality to achieve in human life. Yet God chose the People of Israel to be His 'holy' nation (Exod. 19.6; Deut. 7.6). They were urged to 'be holy, for I am holy' (Lev. 11.44, 45; 19.2). The prophets whose work is recorded in the book of Isaiah looked forward to a time when men would be holy (Isa. 4.3; 62.12). Perhaps Leviticus 20.26 gives the best explanation of what is meant by human holiness: 'You shall be holy to me; for I the LORD am holy, and have separated you from the peoples, that you should be mine.'

We have already seen that the word holiness describes something separated, different, or even strange (see p. 105). Those who have responded to God and are trying to live according to His purposes must be very different from those who have not responded to Him. They will at times seem strange when judged by the standards of those who do not know the LORD. But just as the Holy God makes Himself known to sinful men, so his Holy People must be freely known as a means of blessing to those who do not know the LORD. This is what is meant by the statement that the faithful in Israel are to be priests, representing God among the nations (Isa. 61.6; Exod. 19.6). We must be seen and known to care for all who are in trouble or need, and we must care so much that others come to know God's love through our service.

(b) *Human faithfulness:* God's faithfulness was seen in the fact that He always acts according to His purposes. He is completely reliable in His purposes of steadfast love. Those who put their faith in the LORD will be equally reliable in their relationships with other people. They will always be concerned for the good of their fellows, since they have agreed to follow the lead given by God in His relationships with all men.

Human faithfulness shows itself in a concern for *justice* and *righteousness.* Both these words are often used to translate a single Hebrew word which covers both meanings. We can best distinguish between them by saying that justice is the quality of the actions done by a good man in his relationships with others, while righteousness is the quality of heart which makes such actions possible. See Amos 6.12, where justice is placed in parallel with the fruit of righteousness. The two ideas are set directly in parallel in Isa. 28.17, and Amos 5.24.

The prophets repeatedly complained that there was no justice among men, all their relationships were corrupt (Hab. 1.4). 'Justice is turned back' (Isa. 59.14; compare Isa. 10.2). The prophets urged people not to put their trust in each other because none could be trusted (Mic. 7.2–6; Jer. 9.4–6).

In contrast to this, righteous men serve God (Mal. 3.18), walk in His ways (Hos. 14.9), and do what is lawful (Ezek. 18.5). The thoughts of such men are just (Prov. 12.5), and their words can be trusted (Ps. 37.30; Prov. 10.11, 21). They know the rights of the poor (Prov. 29.7), and are generous (Ps. 37.21; Prov. 21.26). A community that is led by the righteous is a happy one (Prov. 29.2).

(c) *Human steadfast love:* The Hebrew word which is translated 'steadfast love' when used to describe a quality of God, is also used quite often in the Old Testament to describe human relationships. But the scholars who prepared the RSV have almost always avoided using the same English translation in these cases. No doubt they felt that steadfast love was so specially a quality of God that they could not use the same phrase to describe men. Instead, they used the English words 'loyalty' and 'kindness'. In many passages in the RSV Old Testament these two words describe ordinary good human relationships. Abraham, Jonathan, Abner, and David all speak about human 'loyalty' (Gen. 21.23; 1 Sam. 20.15; 2 Sam. 3.8; 10.2). Abraham, Joseph, and Rahab all asked for 'kindness' to be shown to them by their fellows (Gen. 20.13; 40.14; Josh. 2.12).

As the people of Old Testament times began to experience God's steadfast love, they described it by using the best word that they had available. But their experience of God's steadfast love enriched the meaning of the Hebrew word. The scholars who prepared the RSV were right to want to make a distinction between the word as it applied to God, and the word as it was normally understood in human relationships.

But when the prophets came to appreciate the steadfast love of God, they began to teach that God required the same quality in men's relationships with each other. So Micah told his hearers that God requires 'kindness' from His people (Mic. 6.8; compare Zech. 7.9). The Wisdom writers took up the same idea. 'He who withholds kindness from a friend forsakes the fear of the Almighty' (Job 6.14). The word 'loyalty' in Proverbs came to have the same depth of meaning, and could equally well have been translated 'steadfast love' (Prov. 3.3; 16.6; 20.28).

## STUDY SUGGESTIONS

**WORDS**

1. This chapter has been about *relationships*. Which of the following words could best be used instead of the word 'relationship', in the sense in which we use it in this chapter? Which of the words could *not* possibly be used as a substitute?
   alliance  antagonism  association  connection  friendship
2. (a) Explain the differences between the following ways of dying:
   abortion  euthanasia  execution  manslaughter  murder
   (b) To which of them do you think the law, 'you shall not kill', applies? Give reasons for your answer?

**CONTENT**

3. The laws in the Ten Commandments which concern human relationships were qualified and explained by rules contained in the later codes. All were based on the belief that God intends human beings to have happy relationships with each other. Illustrate this from the rules governing sexual relationships.
4. Why did the translators who prepared the RSV avoid using the words 'steadfast love' to express human relationships, while they did use these words to translate the same Hebrew word when it described God's relationship with men?

**BIBLE**

5. Job declared that he had lived righteously (see Job 29.12–17).
   (a) Does Job's idea of righteous behaviour agree with what is written in the book of Deuteronomy?
   (b) For each claim that Job made about having served others, suggest a verse or passage from Deuteronomy that confirms his claim to be righteous. A Concordance will help, e.g. 'poor'— Deuteronomy 15.7.
6. 'Whenever God called someone to serve Him, He did so in order that that person might have an influence within the community in which he lived' (p. 111).
   What sort of influence did God want each of the following men to exert in Israel?
   (a) Elijah     (b) Jeremiah     (c) Nehemiah
7. Read Matthew 5.17–48 and 19.16–22. Then write a paragraph describing the attitude of Jesus to the commandments we have studied in this chapter.

8. 'Ethics are the rules accepted by a community as likely to produce happy and peaceful relationships between the members of that community.'
   Do you think this is an adequate description of:
   (a) the ethics which govern the society in which you live today?
   (b) the ethics of the traditional society of your country?
   (c) the ethics of the Israelite society in Old Testament times?
   Give reasons for your answers.
9. 'Covetousness destroys friendships more quickly than anything else can' (p. 115). What is your opinion? Give your reasons?
10. 'The idea of God is introduced into the discussion of ethics to compel people to obey a morality which has actually been developed from the experience of a human community.' Do you agree with this statement? If so, explain what difference this makes to our interpretation of the Ten Commandments. If not, what evidence can you provide to support your belief that these commandments come from God.

# CHAPTER 7

# The Ultimate Goal

O let the evil of the wicked come to an end,
    but establish thou the righteous,
Thou who triest the minds and hearts,
    thou righteous God.

(Psalm 7.9)

## THE HOPE OF THE RIGHTEOUS

The Psalmists often remarked on the fact that the righteous live among the wicked. Some of the Psalms are a cry for defence against the wicked (e.g. Ps. 10.1, 2; 17.8, 9). Some call on God to judge and punish the wicked (e.g. Pss. 10.15; 28.4). The Psalmists often expressed their confidence that God will deal with people according to their deeds: blessing the righteous, and punishing the wicked (e.g. Pss. 32.10; 34.21, 22). Here then is plenty of evidence that the Jews did not believe that God's plans for His people had reached fulfilment. Some people had turned to God. They had accepted Him as LORD and were glad of their fellowship with Him. These were the righteous. Often they suffered at the hands of the wicked, who refused to serve the LORD. The righteous eagerly looked forward to a future in which God's rule would be seen and accepted in all the earth (Pss. 57.5; 59.13).

For the moment, however, the righteous must live in *hope*, waiting for the day when all God's purposes would be complete. We should notice that the Old Testament idea of hope is very different from the idea of hope in the New Testament, and in Christian doctrine. The reason for the difference is that the Jews had no clear idea of life after death, and no expectation that God's purposes would be fulfilled in a different world from this earthly and physical creation. This was why they placed so much emphasis on personal salvation and the deliverance of the individual from the troubles of this life. The Hebrew word for 'hope' is almost always used in this sense (Ps. 71.5; Prov. 10.28; Job 4.6).

Some Old Testament writers do suggest that there will eventually be some final change when the wicked will be destroyed and the righteous will prosper. These writers realized that life is unsatisfactory, and can never be fully satisfying while the wicked continue to disturb the righteous (Ps. 9.18; Jer. 31.17). But they fail to explain how the righteous who suffer now can share the joys of those future times. The

book of Job emphasizes that the righteous man who suffers hardship
in this world has little hope for the future (Job 7.6; 14.7–10, 19; 17.15);
and in the epilogue, Job's salvation consists in a return to health and
prosperity in this world. There is no guarantee that trouble will not
return.

Yet in the Old Testament hope always goes beyond what can be
expected or explained. People are so fully convinced that God is faithful
and righteous that they find their hope in Him (Ps. 62.1, 2; Job 5.8–16).
Again and again in the Old Testament we find descriptions of what
life will be like one day, when all God's purposes are fulfilled. In taking
a closer look at the nature of these hopes, we must ask 'What did
people expect?', and 'How were these things to be achieved?'

PROPHETIC AND APOCALYPTIC EXPECTATIONS

Many scholars draw our attention to two forms of hope which are
expressed in the Old Testament: the prophetic hope, and the apocalyptic hope. The former is closely related to coming events in the history
of Israel, when God's purposes would be achieved through the work
of individuals and of nations. The latter is based on the belief that
God will intervene in history, and by some dramatic action will bring
evil to an end and establish His rule of righteousness.

The contrast between the two can be seen by comparing the writings
of Deutero-Isaiah with the second part of the book of Daniel. In the
former it is the coming of Cyrus that will bring in the new day of God's
glory (Isa. 45.1–7), while in the latter history is seen as an earthly echo
of events in heaven (Dan. 7.1–14). But the contrast between the two is
not so extreme as some scholars suggest, for on the one hand it is *God*
who has acted in raising up Cyrus, and on the other it is *the saints of
the Most High* who are represented by the 'one like a son of man'.
Both the prophetic and the apocalyptic writings recognize that hope
for the future lies in the hands of God, and that He works his purposes
out through His people.

There is a difference of emphasis, and a difference in the way in
which the message is presented, but no direct conflict of ideas between
the two sorts of writings. This explains the difficulty which scholars
face, in trying to decide how much apocalyptic writing there is contained
in the books of the Old Testament. Some scholars deny that there is
any apart from Daniel, and believe that the real source of apocalyptic
writings is the literature produced in the period between the Old
Testament and the New Testament. Many scholars accept that Isaiah
24—27, Zechariah 9—14, and Daniel 7—12 are apocalyptic writings.
Some scholars see many more such passages in the prophetic books of
the Old Testament. It is significant that apart from Daniel, all the
apocalyptic passages are contained within the prophetic books. If

'God works His purposes out through His people...through human communities. When judgement brought defeat and destruction a few survivors were left to serve Him. Hope for the future was built around a community serving the Lord' (pp. 121, 129). After hospital treatment refugees and wounded survivors of civil war in Africa are given instruction to return to their farms and villages. Volunteer members of 'Operation Brotherhood' in the Philippines work together to bring waste ground into cultivation, as a way of helping the poor. In San Francisco a group of 'Jesus People' rally together to pray for salvation.

For what reasons does a 'community' usually have better hope for the future than isolated individuals?

there had been a real conflict between the messages of the two sorts of writing, it is difficult to see how the apocalyptic passages became part of the prophetic books.

Even the literary styles of the two kinds of writings are not quite so distinctive as some scholars suggest. In Volume 1 of this course (p. 181) the apocalyptic style was described as follows:

> These writers usually recorded their teaching in the form of dreams and visions, which they attributed to important men of past ages. They used these famous names to make the Jews take note of what was written. The names of the authors of these books themselves are mostly unknown.

All the characteristics of the apocalyptic writings can be found in one place or another among the passages which are accepted as being prophetic. The books of Amos, Jeremiah, and especially Ezekiel contain dreams and visions. The book of Jonah is a story which has little to do with the actual life of the man called Jonah, just as the book of Daniel is a story which has little to do with the life of the man called Daniel. The books of Obadiah and Malachi are probably anonymous, their titles simply meaning 'Servant of the LORD' and 'My Messenger' respectively.

Thus there seems to be plenty of evidence to suggest that the apocalyptic writings were a natural development from the earlier prophetic writings, and that the ideas of both concerning hope for the future are closely related. This is what we would expect if we accept the belief that God was leading His people stage by stage to a deeper understanding of His purposes. In the second half of this chapter we shall examine the content of Old Testament hope, and how it was to be achieved. We shall not find it necessary to make a sharp contrast between prophetic and apocalyptic hope.

## STUDY SUGGESTIONS

WORDS

1. This chapter is headed 'The Ultimate Goal'. Which of the following definitions best explains the word 'goal' in that heading?
   (a) A score, as in the game of football,
   (b) The fulfilment, and completion of all that is good,
   (c) The end of the Israelites' journeys in the wilderness.
2. All the following words have some connection with the idea of *hope* as it is used in the English language. Which three are *least* helpful in explaining the biblical idea of hope?
   confidence  desire  dream  expectation  optimism  trust

CONTENT

3. How does the idea of hope in the Old Testament differ from that expressed in the New Testament and in Christian doctrine?

4. What is the most important difference in ideas between prophetic and apocalyptic writings? What is the relationship between the two sets of ideas? Give reasons for your answers.

BIBLE

5. 'God works His purposes out through His people' (p. 121). Does Deutero-Isaiah teach that God's people should wait for the LORD to establish his purposes, or have they a more active part to play in fulfilling his plans for them? (See especially Isa. 45 and 49.)

6. Explain as fully as you can the meaning of Daniel's dream, described in Daniel 7.1–18.

DISCUSSION

7. The Jews of Old Testament times hoped for 'the deliverance of the individual from the troubles of this life' (p. 120). Is this part of the Christian Gospel, and if so, does it differ in any way from the Jewish hope of Old Testament times?

8. Which do you find most helpful as a source of sermon material: Deutero-Isaiah, or the second part of Daniel? Give reasons for your answer.


## WHAT DID THE ISRAELITES EXPECT?

I. THE TRANSFORMATION OF THE PRESENT WORLD

The Jews were realists: they were fully aware of the discomforts and distresses which are part of life in this world. But they did not suppose that these things would continue for ever. They looked forward to a time when people would be freed from them, and would be able to live complete and wholesome lives. Then as now, droughts, blight, and other troubles hindered successful farming and led to hunger. The Jews could not believe that God intended the righteous to suffer in this way; so they looked forward to a time of rich harvests and plenty of food (Amos 9.13–15; Joel 3.18; Ezek. 47.12). Trade with foreign countries would bring prosperity, and poverty would disappear from Israel (Isa. 45.14; 60.11). Troublesome wild animals would be tamed (Isa. 11.6–8; Hos. 2.18), or driven away (Isa. 35.9; Ezek. 34.25; Lev. 26.6). Ill health and crippling disabilities would be cured (Isa. 29.18; 35.5, 6). Since death was regarded as a disaster, some writers promised long life in the new age (Isa. 65.20; Zech. 8.4), and one even believed that death itself would be destroyed (Isa. 25.8). All this would be the

work of God, 'For behold, I create new heavens, and a new earth . . .'
(Isa. 65.17).

## 2. THE ESTABLISHMENT OF A RIGHTEOUS COMMUNITY

In the time of the Exile, the prophets Ezekiel and Deutero-Isaiah
taught the people to look forward to a time when they could return to
Jerusalem. God would be present in the city (Ezek. 43.1–9), and they
would be able to worship Him there for ever (Ezek. 37.26). Earlier
prophecies had prepared the way for those ideas. Judah and Israel
would be reunited (Isa. 11.12, 13; Jer. 3.18), and the people would have
many children to repopulate the land (Jer. 30.18, 19). One early
prophecy which is recorded in two different books had promised that
other nations too would learn to serve the LORD in Jersualem (Isa.
2.2–4; Mic. 4.1–3), and this would bring peace to the world.

After the return from exile, all those ideas were taken up and repeated
by the later prophets, even though the day of the LORD's final victory
over evil had not yet come (e.g. Isa. 52.8; Joel 3.17; Zech. 10.6, 7; 14.16).
These later writings expressed even more clearly the perfection of the
new society to be established in Jerusalem. All the righteous Jews
from all over the world would be gathered there together (Zech. 8.7–9;
Isa. 27.12, 13), people would be gathered from all tribes and nations
to serve the LORD there (Zech. 8.22, 23; Isa. 66.18). The idea that God's
salvation is for all peoples was of course not entirely new. The call of
Abraham had been repeatedly described as a means of blessing for 'all
the families of the earth' (Gen. 12.3; 22.18; 26.4 see RSV footnotes).
Several of the prophets had taken up the idea before the Exile (Zeph.
3.9; Jer. 16.19–21), and others during the Exile (Isa. 45.22; 49.26), in
addition to those after the Exile, as already quoted. Some of the Psalms
express this same idea (Pss. 22.27; 96.9, 10), and it is the main theme of
the books of Ruth and Jonah.

# HOW WAS THIS EXPECTATION TO BE FULFILLED?

The two ideas which together sum up the Old Testament revelation of
how God will achieve His purposes are: (1) the Day of the LORD,
and (2) the One who will come.

## 1. THE DAY OF THE LORD

We noticed the importance of this idea when we were thinking about
God's judgement on sinful men (see p. 81). Now we must examine the
place of that Day in God's creative purposes. It would not, as the People
of Israel imagined, be a day when they would be given glorious
victories over their enemies. They were sinful men, and they would be
judged and punished for what they had done. Yet through God's

activity on that Day a new thing would happen which would establish His rule over His people.

God's activity of judgement would make people recognize that all power, authority, and glory belong to Him. This idea is found in the earliest group of prophetic books (see Isa. 2.10, 19; Amos 8.9, 10; Hos. 2.18–20; Mic. 4.6–7). Look up the word 'know' in a Concordance, and you will see that Ezekiel repeated again and again that on that Day 'they shall know that I am the LORD.' The People of Israel would know it (Ezek. 39.22), and so would all other nations (Ezek. 39.7, 8). Zephaniah took up the idea (Zeph. 3.9), also Deutero-Isaiah (Isa. 52.6), and Joel looked forward to the time when the People of Israel 'shall know that I am the LORD your God' (Joel 3.17).

The apocalyptic chapters of the book of Isaiah make full use of the idea (e.g. Isa. 24.14, 15; 25.9), and the book of Daniel includes a vision of the reign of 'one that was ancient of days', served by a thousand thousand, and with ten thousand times ten thousand standing before him (Dan. 7.9, 10).

Many of the books just quoted describe the Day more fully: the glory of the LORD will be revealed (Isa. 40.5; compare Isa. 28.5; Hab. 2.14); He will reign in Zion (Isa. 24.23; 52.7; Mic. 4.6–7); His majesty will be known among men (Isa. 2.10; 24.14); He shall be exalted (Isa. 2.11; 30.18); men will sing His praises (Isa. 12.5; 24.14; Zech. 2.10; Joel 2.26); 'Out of Zion shall go forth the law, and the word of the LORD from Jerusalem. He shall judge between the nations and shall decide for many peoples' (Isa. 2.3, 4); and in that Day 'All who call upon the name of the LORD shall be delivered' (Joel 2.32).

## 2. THE ONE WHO WILL COME

Many passages in the Old Testament describe how people make use of their past experience of God in order to understand what He will do in the future. They were well aware that God had achieved His purposes in the past by calling men to do His will, and to lead the People of Israel back into His service. So they came to expect that God would send other leaders in the future who would teach them to do God's will, and that God would achieve His purposes for His people through the work of these leaders. Some supposed that an individual would come to carry out God's work among them, some expected that a group of men together would achieve God's purposes.

(a) *Individuals:* The men who prepared the book of Deuteronomy believed that Moses had been a great prophet, speaking to the people in God's name. They expected that God would send other prophets to lead His people (Deut. 18.15–19). They knew from experience that there had been false prophets teaching lies, and they described how these could be distinguished from those who were sent by God (Deut.

18.20–22). But they knew that none of the prophets had served God as faithfully and effectively as Moses had done (Deut. 34.10). The other prophets who would come would have the example of Moses to follow.

Elijah was probably regarded as one of the greatest of the prophets who followed Moses, because of his bold stand against all that was involved in the worship of the Baalim. His greatness was expressed through the belief that he escaped Sheol and entered heaven (2 Kings 2.11). The prophet Malachi looked back to Elijah, and believed that God would send him again to act as herald at the coming of 'the great and terrible day of the LORD' (Mal. 4.5, 6).

Many of the Old Testament writers looked back to the time of David, and remembered his great triumph over Israel's enemies. They remembered the Covenant God had made with David, and they looked forward to a time when a descendant of David would rule in Israel with similar authority and justice. They believed that what God had done once through David, He could do again through the one who would come.

In the meantime, lesser men descended from David would rule over God's people. The prophet Isaiah spoke of one who would come when Ahaz had been defeated by the king of Assyria (Isa. 7.10–17). The same prophet was probably author of the prophecies about a new king in Israel, which we read in Isaiah 9.6, 7 and 11.1–5. Micah made use of similar ideas in writing about the one who would come from Bethlehem, David's home town (Mic. 5.2–4).

Jeremiah, who frequently preached about God's judgement on Israel, looked forward to the coming of a new king of the family of David, who would rule in justice and righteousness (Jer. 23.5, 6). Ezekiel wrote several times about the one whom God would set in authority over His people (Ezek. 17.22; 34.23, 24; 37.22, 24). The prophets who worked in Jerusalem soon after the return from exile looked for the righteous ruler of the house of David, who had been promised so often (Hag. 2.20–23; Zech. 6.9–15). The latest prophecy on the subject was probably Zechariah 9.9, 10.

Notice that the Hebrew word for the one who is to come is never transliterated as 'Messiah' in the RSV Old Testament. The word simply describes people who have been appointed to an office of leadership among the People of Israel *by being anointed.* Anointing was part of the ceremony by which authority was given to those appointed to each of the three chief offices of leadership in Israel. Kings (1 Sam. 10.1, 2) and priests were chosen and anointed (Lev. 8.12), and the prophets too were thought of as having been anointed (Isa. 61.1, and Ps. 105.15). *Messiah,* or 'the LORD's anointed', simply means somebody who has been chosen and appointed to serve the LORD. This is the origin of the Christian use of the word *Messiah,* and also of the word *Christ.* Both

127

'Elijah's greatness was expressed through the belief that he escaped Sheol and entered heaven' (p. 127). Even the Egyptians, who believed in life after death for their Pharaohs and other royal leaders, feared that they might miss this blessing if not properly prepared for it. This picture from the tomb of Tutankhamun shows his successor performing the ritual of 'opening the mouth' so that the dead Pharaoh could receive a new body in the other world, and establish communion between the living and the dead.

titles come from words meaning 'the anointed' in Hebrew and Greek respectively. Jesus is 'the anointed', the One chosen to work for God in bringing salvation to His people.

(b) *A Righteous Group:* Some Old Testament writers hoped for the creation of a righteous community, rather than the coming of an individual leader. No group of people in the history of Israel had been so faithful and effective in the service of God that later writers could remember them as an example of the perfect society that God would re-create in later times. But the fact remained that God had always worked through human communities, e.g. the families of the Patriarchs, the tribes in the time of Moses, the nation in the time of the kings. Even when God's judgement brought defeat and destruction to His people, a few survivors were always left to serve Him. So hope for the future was often built around the idea of a community serving the LORD.

We have already seen that 'the Servant' described by Deutero-Isaiah is best understood as representing the faithful in Israel, who were to be an example to the nations and to other peoples of how God should be served. The suffering of these righteous ones, as they shared in the experiences of the whole nation, could serve to bring salvation to the unfaithful by helping them to understand God's purposes, and His grace.

This same idea of a righteous community serving the LORD probably underlies the vision of the 'Son of Man' in Daniel 7.13, 14. In the earlier part of that chapter the various kingdoms of the world were described as wild beasts, and the Son of Man was coming to rule in their place. The contrast between the individual beasts and the individual Son of Man was meant to show that the new kingdom would be founded on justice and peace, in contrast to the disorder and violence of the earlier kingdoms. But just as each beast had stood for all those who shared in one of the old kingdoms, so the Son of Man stood for all those who would share in the kingdom that was to come. In Daniel 7.18 the new kingdom is said to belong to 'the saints of the Most High'. This is the community which was expected to rule in God's name.

### 3. NEW INTERPRETATIONS

It is important to note that in New Testament times the passages we have been studying in this chapter came to be interpreted in new ways. These new interpretations were made possible by God's fresh revelation of His purposes through the coming of Jesus. In this Guide we have tried to understand the hopes of the Jewish people at the end of the Old Testament period, recognizing that God's work of revelation was not yet completed. Remembering this, we shall find it easier to understand why the Jewish people did not immediately recognize that the coming of Jesus was the fulfilment of all that God had promised to

His people in Old Testament times. They had learnt to look forward to a new activity of God among His people, but they were not fully aware of how it would happen. They believed, and still believe, that He would in some way establish His rule over all men in justice and righteousness. The Incarnation of the Son of God was a mystery too deep for the most profound and faithful men to understand, except, as Paul said, 'in a mirror dimly . . . in part' (1 Cor. 13.12).

## STUDY SUGGESTIONS

WORDS

1. 'Thine, O LORD, is the greatness, and the power, and the glory, and the victory, and the majesty' (1 Chron. 29.11).
   What other words can you find used in the Old Testament alongside the word 'majesty', to express the same or similar ideas? Give at least three words, and the verses where they occur.
2. Which one of the following words best explains the meaning of the word 'kingdom' in the phrase 'kingdom of God'?
   country    inhabitants    nationality    population    **rule**    territory

CONTENT

3. 'Many passages in the Old Testament describe how people make use of their past experience of God in order to understand what He will do in future' (p. 126).
   Give examples of how your own experiences have affected your beliefs about the future.
4. Isaiah 2.2–4; 27.12, 13, and 52.8 are all quoted in this chapter. Are these passages thought to be the work of one prophet, or more than one? Describe the origin of each passage so far as you know it.

BIBLE

5. 'Be exalted, O God' (Ps. 21.13). The word 'exalted' means literally to be lifted up. In what sense did the biblical writers think of God being exalted?
6. What has Deutero-Isaiah to say about the future of Jerusalem? (Remember that 'Zion' is an alternative name for Jerusalem.) Include in your answer, information from the chapters of Isaiah which were probably written in Jerusalem after the Exile.

DISCUSSION

7. What use of the Old Testament idea of the transformation of the present world should we make in our preaching, and our faith?

8. What ideas about the ultimate goal of all things are part of the traditional religion of your people? How do these ideas differ from the ideas of Old Testament writers? Which group of ideas provides the most helpful basis for the study of New Testament ideas among your people?
9. How would you answer if somebody asked you what are the Christian ideas of the ultimate goal of all things?
10. How far is it helpful to try to understand Old Testament ideas in separation from their New Testament interpretation?
   Do Old Testament passages really have two different meanings:
   (a) the meaning they had for the people who wrote and read them in the Old Testament times, and
   (b) the meaning that Christians can see in them through the great light which shines on God's purposes because of the coming of Jesus?
   If so, does this mean that Old Testament writers were unaware of the full significance of what they wrote?

# CHAPTER 8

# The Old Testament in the New Testament

## A GROWING PLANT

The Bible can be compared with a growing plant, such as a rose. The Old Testament is like the root, stem, leaves, and calyx. The New Testament is like the blossom, the crowning glory of the plant. The Holy Spirit is like the sap running through the plant and bringing life to every part.

Biblical Theology is like botany. It is the study of the nature of the Bible, just as botany is the study of the nature of the plant. Old Testament Theology is like that part of botany which describes the whole supporting system of a plant's life that makes its flowering possible. It is an attempt to describe the knowledge and understanding that came to men through God's continuing work of revelation. It shows what went before and supports the revelation of God in Christ Jesus.

Some scholars study the Theology of the Old Testament from its beginnings, describing in detail each stage of its growth. This is like a botanist describing the development of a flower by starting from its seed, and following every stage of the plant's development till it is fully grown and ready to produce its blossom. We studied Old Testament religion in this way in the first volume of this course. The third section of each chapter of that book describes the religious practices of God's People as they developed, stage by stage, throughout the history of Israel. But this was much easier to do than it is to describe the development of Old Testament Theology in the same way. The outward forms of religious activity are more easily recognized and recorded than the inward realities of theological thought.

The botanist can see a plant at each stage of its growth, and describe its development as it takes place. He would find it more difficult to describe each stage of growth merely by looking at the full grown plant, though some things would be obvious from the final form to which it developed. The Old Testament as we know it is at its final stage of growth, and we have similar problems in trying to describe how it grew. Even though there is a wide range of books in the Old Testament, recording the thoughts of writers of those times, we do not know exactly when each was written, or which parts of each book are later additions, containing later ideas. Some things stand out clearly enough, but other things are obscure. So in this volume we have tried to describe the full grown Theology of the Old Testament, and to show the most obvious evidence of development of thought as we have dealt with each part of it.

We could in this chapter go on to describe the Theology of the New Testament, just a botanist would go on to describe the blossom, and the part it plays in the life of the plant. But in order to do this we should need to study the history of the New Testament period, and the origin and content of the books of the New Testament. It would involve such far-ranging study that the chapter would become another book. So we do not attempt to study New Testament Theology in this volume, but leave it to other authors, and to other books.

As a preparation for that study, the purpose of this chapter is to examine the connection between the Old Testament and the New Testament. This connection is just as important as that between a blossom and the plant on which it grew. A vase of cut flowers may look very beautiful, but the blossoms have ceased to grow, and will never produce seeds leading to new life. If the New Testament is to be properly understood and appreciated it must not be cut off from the richness of its association with the Old Testament. God has been revealing Himself throughout history, and He still makes Himself known to us through the whole record of His activities in Israel. If we separate the New Testament from the Old Testament, and study the revelation of God in Christ Jesus apart from the whole record of how God has made Himself known to men, we hinder our understanding of God and the world, and of man and his destiny. What then are the living connections between the two parts of the Bible?

## DIRECT QUOTATIONS

It is not always easy to see how Old Testament ideas have affected the thinking of New Testament writers. These writers do not always say exactly how they came to understand God's purposes and God's activities in the way that they did. Because the New Testament writers were Christians, the most important influence in all their thinking is that of Jesus Christ Himself: what He was, what He did, and what He taught. But there is plenty of evidence in the writings of the New Testament to show that they were able to understand and appreciate the importance of Jesus Christ, and of His teachings, because they were already aware of all that God had revealed in Old Testament times. This evidence is clearest where the writers quote verses from the Old Testament to help them explain the new revelation that had come in Christ Jesus. They were leading their readers along the same paths towards understanding as they had travelled themselves.

There are several ways in which we can discover these quotations in order to see how New Testament writers used Old Testament ideas:

'If the New Testament is to be properly understood and appreciated, it must
be seen in all the richness of its association with the Old Testament' (p. 133).
The early Christians, following the example of Jesus Christ, made great use of
religious symbols from Old Testament times. This picture shows part of the
carving on a stone sarcophagus (coffin) of the third century AD. The Good
Shepherd is clearly portrayed in the centre, and the background is part of a
grape-harvest scene, reminding us of the important part played by the Vine
in biblical thought.

(a) In the RSV and many other modern translations of the Bible much of the Old Testament is printed in the style of poetry, based on the poetic forms of the Hebrew writings, e.g. most of the prophetic writings, Psalms, and Proverbs. None of the New Testament books are written mainly in poetry. It only appears from time to time in the middle of prose writing. Sometimes this poetry is a new expression of praise to God, as in Revelation 4.11 and 5.9, 10. But most of the poetry in the New Testament is in fact quoted from the Old Testament. For example, Hebrews 1, 5–13 is composed of quotations from six Psalms, and from 2 Samuel and Deuteronomy (see the RSV footnotes).

(b) In the RSV and some other versions, footnotes are included which draw our attention to quotations from the Old Testament, whether or not they are poetic in form. So this is another source of information about quotations, although some of the footnotes draw our attention to similar ideas in other parts of the Bible rather than direct quotations.

(c) A Concordance can help us too, especially as quotations are often introduced by such phrases as 'Have you not read . . .' (Matt. 12.3, 5), and 'It is written . . .' (Luke 20.17; 24.46). In several cases an event is described as fulfilling what is written in the Old Testament (Matt. 13.14; John 19.28).

## I. THE USE OF THE SEPTUAGINT

If we make a careful comparison between the quotations as they stand in the New Testament, and the actual verses as they appear in the Old Testament, we find that in many cases the wording differs, for example Matthew 13.14 reads:

'You shall indeed hear but never understand,
and you shall indeed see but never perceive.'

This is a quotation of Isaiah 6.9, which reads:

'Hear and hear, but do not understand;
See and see, but do not perceive.'

The difference comes from the fact that the Old Testament was written in Hebrew, and the New Testament in Greek. The New Testament writers did not normally use the Hebrew books which later formed the Jewish scriptures, and they did not normally make their own translation into Greek. Instead, they used the Septuagint, a Greek translation of the books of the Old Testament and Apocrypha, which had been prepared by Jews and was widely used by Jewish communities away from Palestine (see Vol. 2, pp. 9, 10). The New Testament writers used this version because it would help to persuade these Jews that the Christian

Gospel was directly related to what they already knew about God and His purposes from their study of the Septuagint.

The Scholars who prepared the RSV translated directly from the Greek of the New Testament books, and this explains the differences between these quotations and their Old Testament sources. Often the differences are only slight, as in the example already given. But sometimes there is a more significant difference. For example, Matthew 1.23 refers to a 'virgin' who shall conceive. In the Old Testament it is a 'young woman' who shall do so (Isa. 7.14). The Hebrew word simply means a woman of the age to be married, and does not show whether she is married or not. The Greek word used in the Septuagint means a virgin, and cannot be used of a married woman. So this verse has changed in an important way when it reappears in the New Testament. Those who prepared the Septuagint are responsible for the change, and have introduced the idea of a miracle to the passage.

## 2. FULFILMENT OF PROPHECY

It is sometimes difficult for us to understand how an event in New Testament times can be regarded as a fulfilment of prophecies recorded in the Old Testament. The verse we have just examined is a good example. Isaiah was quite clearly referring to events near to his own time, after the death of Ahaz and before the Assyrians attacked Judah: 'Before the child knows how to refuse the evil and choose the good, the land before whose two kings you are in dread will be deserted . . .' (Isa. 7.16). Yet the writer of Matthew says of the birth of Jesus; 'All this took place to fulfil what the LORD had spoken by the prophet' (Matt. 1.22).

The connection between the prophecy and the event recorded in the New Testament was not a directly historical one. Isaiah was not promising to Ahaz something that would happen many centuries later, long after his enemies and the Assyrians had been destroyed. But there is a real theological link. Isaiah was confident that God would not leave his people without a worthy leader to teach them how to serve Him. Ahaz had failed, but another would come, who would share in the consequences of Ahaz's sins, yet would Himself live righteously in the new circumstances of God's People. Many centuries later Jesus was born as the One above all others who would be a worthy leader for God's People, sharing their sufferings and showing them true righteousness.

Many of the verses quoted from the Old Testament actually refer to moments in history earlier than the time of Christ and of the early Church. We shall only understand these quotations aright if we can recognize their theological meaning, and distinguish it from their historical associations.

Now we are ready to examine the quotations used in the New Testament in more detail. First we shall consider the way in which Jesus used the Old Testament, then how the Apostle Paul did, and finally the other New Testament writers.

## 3. HOW JESUS USED THE OLD TESTAMENT

The Old Testament had a very important place in the personal life of Jesus. When He described to His disciples His experience of temptation at the beginning of His ministry, He explained it in terms of Old Testament quotations. Both the Devil and Jesus Himself referred to the Scriptures during that great conflict of their wills (Matt. 4.1-11; Luke 4.1-13). Similarly, at His crucifixion, Jesus found strength to face the suffering through words from the Old Testament. His cry from the cross, 'Why hast thou forsaken me?', is a direct quotation of Psalm 22.1. Many other verses in that Psalm can be used to describe the experience of crucifixion, e.g. 'They have pierced my hands and my feet' (v. 16). And the Psalmist's confidence in God's power to deliver may even have served to reassure Jesus. Certainly His cry at the moment of death was an expression of trust and confidence in God (see Luke 23.46), and was quoted from Psalm 31.5.

Jesus was concerned too that His followers should understand and benefit from God's revelation of Himself as recorded in the Old Testament. Some people have suggested that there is a conflict of ideas in Jesus's teaching, regarding the relationship between the Old Testament and His own ministry. He said on the one hand 'I have come not to abolish the law and the prophets but to fulfil them' (Matt. 5.17). Yet on the other hand He compared His ministry to new cloth, and new wine, which must not be used to mend old cloth, or to fill old wine skins (Matt. 9.16, 17).

However, the contrast is not so complete as it seems. The Old Testament finds its fulfilment in the New Testament. It is incomplete in itself, and does not present a full account of God's revelation. It must not be used to prevent people from seeing the fuller truth revealed in Christ, but to help them to understand and appreciate the New Testament revelation.

Jesus made use of all three parts of the Hebrew Scriptures in His teachings.

1. He pointed out the two *Laws* which are a basis for understanding all that God requires of His people (Mark 12.29-31; Matt. 22.37-40). He approved the Ten Commandments as a guide for life (Mark 10.19-21), and added His own fuller interpretation to ensure that His disciples understood their real meaning and importance (Matt. 5.21-37).

2. He used the *Prophets* to explain the purpose and significance of

His own ministry (Luke 4.18, 19; compare Isa. 61.1, 2). 'It is written in the prophets, and they shall all be taught by God' (John 6.45, compare Isa. 54.13). 'And he was reckoned with transgressors' (Luke 22.37, compare Isa. 53.12).

3. He used the *Psalms*, which are part of the Writings, to explain the significance of His own sufferings. 'He who ate my bread has lifted up his heel against me' (John 13.18; compare Ps. 41.9), and 'They hated me without a cause' (John 15.25; compare Ps. 35.19). He claimed to be the stone that the builders had rejected (Luke 20.17; compare Ps. 118.22–23).

Jesus also tried to prepare His disciples for His sufferings, by showing them that it was a fulfilment of what was written in all the Scriptures (Mark 9.12; Luke 18.31–34). He returned to the same subject at the Last Supper (Mark 14.21), and at His arrest (Matt. 26.54–56). His meaning became clear to His disciples after His resurrection, on the road to Emmaus and in Jerusalem (Luke 24.27, 44).

## 4. PAUL AND THE OLD TESTAMENT

The first Christian writings were the letters of Paul. He had been a Pharisee, and was trained in the Jewish way of understanding what we call the Old Testament. As a Pharisee he had learnt to value the Scriptures very highly, so it is not surprising that in these circumstances he often mentioned them in his letters. Wherever he went on his travels he spoke first to the Jews and the proselytes, and only afterwards to the Gentiles. As a result, many of the early converts to Christianity were people who knew the Septuagint very well, and could benefit from their knowledge as they heard Paul preach or read his letters.

Paul's letter to the Romans provided an excellent example of the way in which he used the Old Testament to support what he was saying. The chart on p. 139 shows Paul's quotations from the Law, the Prophets, and the Writings, set out in the order in which they appear in the letter. The large number of the quotations, and the fact that they are drawn from many different parts of the Old Testament, show that Paul had an extensive knowledge of the Scriptures, and did not hesitate to use them as evidence of what God had revealed about Himself and His purposes for men.

When we look more closely at these same quotations, we find that they include all the most important ideas covered by Old Testament Theology. They describe the nature of God, and the quality and character of His relationship with men.

God has made Himself known to men (Deut. 30.12, 14;) He is wise (Isa. 40.13, 14), and just (Deut. 10.17; 2 Chron. 19.7; Ps. 51.4). He has the right to be served by all men (Isa. 45.23), and His authority is shown even in His relationships with those who are disobedient

**Paul's use of Old Testament quotations in his Letter to the Romans**

| Rom: | The Law | Rom: | The Prophets | Rom: | The Writings |
|---|---|---|---|---|---|
| | | 1.17 | Hab. 2.4 | | |
| 2.11 | Deut. 10.17 | 2.24 | Isa. 52.5 | 2.11 | 2 Chron. 19.7 |
| | | | | 3.4 | Psalm 51.4 |
| | | | | 3.10-12 | Pss. 14.1-3; 53.1-3 |
| | | | | 3.13 | Pss. 5.9; 140.3 |
| | | | | 3.14 | Psalm 10.7 |
| | | 3.15-17 | Isa. 59.7, 8 | 3.18 | Psalm 36.1 |
| | | | | 3.20 | Psalm 143.2 |
| 4.3 | Gen. 15.6 | | | 4.7 | Psalm 32.1, 2 |
| 4.17 | Gen. 17.5 | | | | |
| 4.18 | Gen. 15.5 | | | | |
| 7.7 | Exod. 20.17; | | | 7.22 | Psalm 1.2 |
| | Deut. 5.21 | | | 8.31 | Psalm 118.6 |
| | | 8.33 | Isa. 50.8, 9 | 8.36 | Psalm 44.22 |
| 9.7 | Gen. 21.12 | | | | |
| 9.9 | Gen. 18.10 | | | | |
| 9.12 | Gen. 25.23 | 9.13 | Mal. 1.2, 3 | 9.14 | 2 Chron. 19.7 |
| 9.15 | Exod. 33.19 | | | | |
| 9.17 | Exod. 9.16 | 9.20 | Isa. 45.9 | | |
| | | 9.25 | Hos. 2.23 | | |
| | | 9.26 | Hos. 1.10 | | |
| | | 9.27 | Isa. 10.22, 23; Hos. 1.10 | | |
| | | 9.29 | Isa. 1.9 | | |
| | | 9.33 | Isa. 28.16 | | |
| 10.5 | Lev. 18.5 | 10.5 | Ezek. 20.11 | 10.5 | Neh. 9.29 |
| 10.6 | Deut. 30.12 | | | | |
| 10.8 | Deut. 30.14 | 10.11 | Isa. 28.16 | | |
| | | 10.13 | Joel 2.32 | | |
| | | 10.15 | Isa. 52.7 | | |
| | | 10.16 | Isa. 53.1 | 10.18 | Psalm 19.4 |
| 10.19 | Deut. 32.21 | 10.20,21 | Isa. 65.1, 2 | | |
| | | 11.3,4 | 1 Kings 19.10, 18 | | |
| | | 11.8 | Isa. 29.10 | 11.9 | Psalm 69.22,23 |
| | | 11.26 | Isa. 59.20,21 | | |
| | | 11.34 | Isa. 40.13,14 | 11.35 | Job 41.11 |
| 12.19 | Deut. 32.35 | | | 12.20 | Prov. 25.21,22 |
| 13.9 | Exod. 20.13 - 17; Deut. 5.17,18; Lev. 19.18 | | | | |
| | | 14.11 | Isa. 45.23 | | |
| | | | | 15.3 | Psalm 69.9 |
| | | 15.9 | 2 Sam. 22.50; | 15.9 | Psalm 18.49 |
| 15.10 | Deut. 32.43 | | | | |
| | | | | 15.11 | Psalm 117.1 |
| | | 15.12 | Isa. 11.10 | | |
| | | 15.21 | Isa. 52.15 | | |

(Exod. 9.16). His laws help men to know how they should live (Lev. 18.5; Ezek. 20.11; Ps. 1.2). He will judge disobedient men (Isa. 28.16); and punish their wrongdoing (Deut. 32.35). Yet God is merciful (Exod. 33.19), and works for men's salvation (Isa. 52.7; Joel 2.32); His goodness to men has not been bought (Job 41.11); man's hope springs from God's willingness to forgive (Ps. 32.1, 2).

None can stand secure under God's judgement (Ps. 143.2), because all have been disobedient and have sinned (Pss. 5.9; 14.1–3), but God has provided a way of salvation: Abraham was accepted because of his faith (Gen. 15.6), and others can follow the same way (Hab. 2.4). God chose the People of Israel (Mal. 1.2, 3); but even they rejected His choice of them (Isa. 45.9) and refused to hear His messengers (1 Kings 19.10). Yet God went on seeking a response from His people (Isa. 65.1, 2), and continually renewed His election of Israel (Isa. 59.20, 21; Hos. 1.10; 2.23); there would be a remnant who would respond to Him (1 Kings 19.18; Isa. 1.9; 10.22, 23), and they would be a witness to all people of God's goodness to men (Ps. 19.4; Isa. 11.10; 52.15). Eventually God's promises to Abraham would be fulfilled (Gen. 15.5; 17.5); men would live according to God's will as described in the Ten Commandments (Exod. 20.13–17); they would learn to love their neighbours (Lev. 19.18), and to show kindness to their enemies (Prov. 25.21, 22).

Paul's letter to the Romans was addressed to the Church in Rome, whose members included Jews and gentile converts to Judaism, who had become Christians. Such people would be greatly helped by Paul's use of the Old Testament, which was well known to them all. But we must not make the mistake of supposing that Paul used Old Testament quotations just because his hearers were familiar with them. Paul himself had come to Christian faith after being a student of the Old Testament. Paul's meeting with Christ on the road to Damascus was a completion and fulfilment of all that he had come to know about God through his study of the Law, the Prophets, and the Writings. It was natural for him to make use of the Old Testament ideas, because they were deeply involved in his own understanding of the Christian Gospel. He wanted his hearers to share the same benefits that he himself had found.

## 5. OTHER WRITERS

We cannot in this volume study in such detail the work of other writers who contributed to the New Testament. But one or two examples will show how they valued the Old Testament because it provided familiar passages which enabled them to express their message about the coming of Christ in ways that would appeal to their readers.

(a) The writers of the Gospels made it clear that they found this useful (Luke 3.4–6; John 12.15), and Matthew used a series of quotations to show that the life of Jesus was a fulfilment of prophecy (Matt. 1.22; 2.15; 2.23; 8.17; 12.17–21; 13.35; 21.4). Some scholars have even suggested that the early Church had a collection of such texts drawn up as a help in presenting the Gospel to the Jews. This may have been necessary for Christian teachers, who were not so well acquainted with the Old Testament as Paul showed himself to be. Most of these quotations are not taken from the Septuagint.

(b) The writer of the letter to the Hebrews used Old Testament ideas of priesthood, sanctuary, and sacrifice to express what he believed Jesus had accomplished by His death and resurrection. His letter also refers to the work of Moses, and to the New Covenant. He especially, among the New Testament writers, used many quotations from the Old Testament, which are all given in detail in the footnotes of the RSV, and most of which stand out from the prose of the letter because of their poetic form.

## STUDY SUGGESTIONS

WORDS

1. 'If the New Testament is to be properly understood and appreciated, it must not be cut off from the richness of its association with the Old Testament' (p. 133). Which one of the following words best expresses the meaning of *appreciated* in that sentence?
   assessed   confirmed   criticized   digested   honoured   increased
2. 'In several cases an event is described as fulfilling what is written in the Old Testament' (p. 135). An example of this is found in John 19.23, 24. Which of the following explanations best shows what the word 'fulfil' means in this example?
   (a) Because the Psalmist had said that lots would be cast the soldiers found themselves compelled to do so.
   (b) The Psalmist had experienced the indignity of having his clothes divided among his persecutors, and yet had not despaired of God's protection. When Jesus was faced by similar suffering, He fulfilled the Scriptures by showing similar faith in God. Neither were ever beyond God's care.
   (c) God had seen beforehand what would happen, and had made it known to the Psalmist. When it happened the disciples knew that this was what God had already revealed.

CONTENT

3. Why did New Testament writers make use of the Septuagint rather than the Hebrew Scriptures? What exception to this do you know about?

4. In what two chief ways did Jesus make use of quotations from the Old Testament? Give three examples of each.

BIBLE

5. Assuming that the RSV provides a good translation of the meaning of both Zechariah 9.9, and Matthew 21.5, can you suggest how it was that Matthew supposed that Jesus rode on two animals when he entered Jerusalem on Palm Sunday?

6. Many of the references to the Old Testament in the RSV footnotes to Paul's letter to the Romans are omitted on the chart on p. 139 because they do not relate to direct quotations. What is the significance of these other references? To show the accuracy of your answer, choose three good examples, and set the New Testament verse side by side with the Old Testament verse.

DISCUSSION

7. Why did the New Testament writers quote the Old Testament so frequently? In what way does your answer affect your own attitude to the use of the Old Testament in the life of the Church today?

8. There are no references to the Old Testament in the RSV footnotes to Paul's letter to the Philippians. Can you suggest why this is so? Does it make any difference to the belief that Paul found it necessary to use Old Testament quotations in order to express New Testament Theology?

## OTHER REFERENCES

I. PEOPLE, PLACES, AND CUSTOMS

There are many other references to the Old Testament in the books of the New Testament, besides the direct quotations we have already noticed. The most obvious examples are references to people, places, and customs whose importance is made clear by study of the Old Testament.

(a) *People:* About fifty names of people mentioned in the Old Testament appear also in the New Testament. Many of these names appear in the lists of Joseph's ancestors (Matt. 1.1–17; Luke 3.23–38). Their names help to express the Gospel writers' belief that Jesus was a true successor to those who had led Israel in God's name in earlier times. They show that His coming was a fulfilment of God's activities among His people, in all ages from the time of Abraham. Other people are mentioned as the founder members of the tribes of Israel (see especially Revelation 7.4–8). These references, too, are meant to show the fulfilment of all that God had begun through these children of Jacob. Paul, for example, was proud of the fact that he belonged to the tribe of Benjamin (Rom. 11.1, Phil. 3.5).

But the most important of these people are those who are mentioned again and again in the New Testament. They included the following (the figures in brackets show the number of times their names appear in the New Testament): Adam (9 times), Noah (8), Abraham (74), Isaac (19), Jacob (25), Joseph (9), Moses (79), David (58), Solomon (12), Elijah (30), Isaiah (21), and Jonah (9).

Those who heard Jesus or one of the apostles preach, and those who read a New Testament letter or a Gospel, needed to have a sound knowledge of Old Testament history in order to appreciate these allusions. The early Christian preachers and teachers knew that such knowledge was available to the Jews and proselytes, because the Scriptures were regularly taught and expounded in the synagogues in those days. Christians believed that they could make their own message clear to their hearers by referring to these people of past ages, and to what they had experienced of God in their own day. The New Testament preachers and writers used the sound educational principle of using the existing knowledge of their hearers, and of building on it fresh understanding and new knowledge of God's ways.

(b) *Places:* The events of the New Testament happened in much the same part of the world as those recorded in the Old Testament. Palestine was at the centre and background of both histories; its towns and villages are mentioned in both parts of the Bible. A well-trained Jew would remember Old Testament stories about places which were in the news in his own time because of the activities of Jesus and his followers. For example, Jerusalem would always be thought of as the City of David, and the fact that one of David's descendants was active there would rouse interest in any loyal Jewish heart.

The fact that David's descendant was rejected and crucified there by the Jewish people would cause horror and despair to those who believed that Jesus was sent by God, because God's people had turned against the LORD's Anointed. The Jewish Christians would remember other members of their race who had suffered there as a result of the disloyalty of God's people, e.g. Jeremiah and the Maccabees. Christ's warnings about the coming destruction of Jerusalem would remind them of Isaiah's assurance that Jerusalem would never be destroyed, and of the dismay caused by Jeremiah's certainty that it would, and by the fact that it *had* in fact been destroyed. If God could reject the Jews so completely in the time of Jeremiah, then it might well happen again, as Jesus was predicting. In the minds of the Jews in New Testament times, the background of Old Testament experience and thought was firmly associated with the places involved in the story of the life and ministry of Jesus. The New Testament writers made full use of these associations in presenting their message to the people of their day.

Here are a few other examples: Bethlehem had been important, and

143

would be again (Matt. 2.3–6). Nowhere in all the journey back from exile was there greater need for valleys to be lifted up, and mountains made low, than in the Jordan valley (Isa. 40.3–5), and it was here that John the Baptist preached about another new beginning for God's people (Matt. 3.1–3).

Samaria had been capital of the Northern Kingdom, as well as the source of opposition to the re-establishment of God's people in Jerusalem after the Exile. If God's rule was to be established, the people of Samaria must be won to the service of God (John 4.39–42; Acts 8.4–8).

Galilee had been a remote part of the kingdom of Israel, easily conquered (2 Kings 15.29), and had even been given away in a trade agreement (1 Kings 9.11). But Isaiah had believed that it would have an important part and place in God's plans for all His people (Isa. 9.1). The fact that a great part of Jesus's ministry was exercised in Galilee, was no matter for surprise, but simply what had been expected for the place (Matt. 4.12–17).

(c) *Customs:* The customs observed by the Jewish people in New Testament times had developed over the whole period of their history from the time of Abraham to the time of Christ. The various stages of this development are recorded in the Old Testament, and New Testament writers refer to many of these customs as they record the life and teaching of Jesus, or describe the growth of the Christian Church and its relations with the Jewish community.

The most obvious example is that of circumcision. The Jerusalem Council and Paul's letter to the Galatians were largely concerned with whether or not Gentiles should be circumcised before they could be accepted as Christian converts. The answer they gave is a matter for New Testament Theology, and we are only concerned here to notice the Old Testament background to the dispute. Circumcision for the Jews began in the time of Abraham (Gen. 17.9–14), and became a sign for those who shared in God's covenant with Israel. Jesus himself was circumcised (Luke 2.21), and Paul expressed the pride felt by all Jews in belonging to those who were circumcised (Phil. 3.5). But even in Old Testament times, they recognized that the outward sign had no meaning without a corresponding attitude of heart and mind (Jer. 4.4, 9.25, 26). When circumcision was eventually declared unnecessary for Gentiles, it was a natural sequel of this development of ideas. The truly circumcised are those 'who worship God in spirit, and glory in Christ Jesus, and put no confidence in the flesh' (Phil. 3.3).

Other religious customs described in the New Testament, which depend for their explanation and significance on the Old Testament, include: the appointment of priests (Matt. 8.4); the observance of the Sabbath (Matt. 12.2), fasts (Matt. 6.16), and annual feasts (Luke 2.41);

the giving of tithes (Matt. 23.23), and the making of sacrifices (Luke 2.24); teaching in the synagogues (Matt. 4.23); and the wearing of phylacteries (Matt. 23.5). We can only understand these references when we know the origin and purpose of the customs involved. This knowledge comes to us from a study of the Old Testament.

## 2. THEMES

The most important influence of the Old Testament on the writings of the New Testament is seen in the way in which theological themes are taken up and used afresh in presenting the Gospel. The whole purpose of God's revelation in the Old Testament was that people should learn about Him and enter into fellowship with Him. Those who knew the LORD were eager to share their experiences with others, so that they might experience the same joy.

In passing on their knowledge of God to others, the Old Testament writers built up a vocabulary of special words and phrases which their hearers would find helpful in trying to understand their message. These same words and phrases were used by Jesus, and by other people of His times, to express the truth of God's new revelation of Himself in Christ. It is easy to find examples of the way in which the Old Testament vocabulary was used to present the New Testament message. They can be found on every page of the New Testament. Simply as an example, a few of these references are given in the chart on p. 146. It is not intended to be complete, either in its list of Old Testament themes, or in its list of verses from the New Testament where these themes are taken up again.

Careful study of these examples will show that the New Testament writers were not merely repeating Old Testament ideas. Although they used the same words and phrases, the meaning which they expressed through them was different. It was changed and enlarged because of the coming of Jesus Christ. What He had been, and said, and done, enriched and transformed men's understanding of God and His purposes.

The Old Testament vocabulary came to have new meanings as a result. To take one example only, the idea of the unity of God now includes the existence of Father and Son together as One (John 10.30; 17.22, etc.). We cannot in this book study all such changes, not can we study the whole range of new understanding which resulted from the coming of Christ. This is the study of New Testament Theology. But without the Old Testament vocabulary, the new knowledge could not have been expressed in terms that would be appreciated by those who were hearing the Gospel for the first time. And we still use that vocabulary today.

There is not a single page of the New Testament which can be

**Examples of Old Testament themes referred to in the New Testament**

| Chapter in Guide | O.T. Theme | New Testament references |
|---|---|---|
| Introd: The Word of God | Inspiration<br>Revelation | 2 Tim. 3.16;  Heb. 1.1, 2<br>Matt. 11.25-27;  16.17;  1 Cor. 2.9, 10;<br>Eph. 3.4-6 |
| 1. God | Unity of God<br><br>Creation<br>Purpose in history<br>Righteousness | John 10.30;  17.22;  Rom. 3.30;  1 Cor. 8.6;<br>Eph. 4.6<br>Mark 10.6;  John 1.3;  Col. 1.16<br>Eph. 3.8-12<br>Matt. 6.33;  Rom. 3.21-26;  Gal. 3.21 |
| 2. Other Spiritual Beings | Angels<br>Satan | Luke 1.30;  John 20.12;  2 Thes. 1.7; Rev.8.2<br>Mark 1.13;  Luke 10.18;  Rom. 16.20;<br>Rev. 12.9 |
| 3. Man | Image of God<br>Flesh<br>Soul<br>Spirit<br>Sheol<br>Resurrection | 1 Cor. 11.7;  Col. 3.10<br>Matt. 26.41;  John 1.14<br>Matt. 10.28;  1 Cor. 15.45<br>John 3.6;  Rom. 8.16<br>1 Pet. 3.19<br>Matt. 22.28;  John 5.28, 29;  Rom. 6.5 |
| 4. The Fall | Temptation<br><br>Sin<br>Wrath<br>Judgment | Matt. 6.13;  Mark 14.38;  1 Cor. 10.13;<br>Heb. 2.18<br>Luke 15.18, 21;  John 8.11;  Rom. 2.12<br>Matt. 3.7;  John 3.36;  Rom. 1.18;  Rev. 6.17<br>Matt. 10.15;  John 5.22-24;  1 Tim. 5.24;<br>Rev. 14.7 |
| 5. Salvation | Steadfast love<br>Covenant<br>Sacrifice | John 3.16;  15.9;  Eph. 2.4, 5; 1 John 4.10,11<br>1 Cor.11.25;  2 Cor. 3.4-6;  Heb. 12.18-24<br>Rom. 12.1;  Eph. 5.1,2;  Heb. 9.23-28 |
| 6. The New Life | Fear of God<br>Faith in God<br>Love for God<br>Love for others | Matt. 10.28;  Acts 10.2;  Col. 3.22; Rev. 14.7<br>Mark 11.22;  Luke 7.9;  Rom. 4.5;  Eph. 2.8<br>Matt. 22.37;  Rom. 8.28;  1 John 4.19<br>Matt. 5.43-45;  John 13.34;  Rom. 13.8;<br>1 John 4.7 |
| 7. The Ultimate Goal | Transformation of the world<br>New Community<br>Day of the Lord<br>Son of Man | Rom. 8.19-21;  2 Pet. 3.13;  Rev. 21.1-4<br><br>1 Cor. 15.20-28;  Col. 1.18;  Rev. 7.9-12<br>Matt. 11.22-24;  1 Cor. 1.7, 8;  Heb. 10.25<br>Matt. 16.27;  26.64;  Rev. 14.14 |

properly understood without knowing the background of experience and thought which is recorded in the Old Testament. The New Testament writers were fully aware of their dependence on the Old Testament in trying to express God's new revelation in Jesus Christ in ways that men could understand and appreciate. Jesus Himself made full use of the Old Testament revelation, because He knew that all through history God had been preparing people's minds and hearts for the time of His coming. 'When the time had fully come, God sent forth His Son' (Gal. 4.4). In every generation Christians must come to grips with all that was revealed in Old Testament times, if they are to know the full significance of Christ's coming.

## STUDY SUGGESTIONS

WORDS

1. Which one of the following words best expresses the meaning of the word 'themes', as used in a subheading on p. 145?
   arguments   problems   propositions   subjects   texts
2. Which of the following definitions (taken from *The Advanced Learner's Dictionary*) best expresses the meaning of the word 'customs' as used on p. 144?
   (a) usual and generally accepted behaviour among members of a social group
   (b) regular support given to a tradesman by those who buy his goods
   (c) taxes due to the government on goods imported into a country

CONTENT

3. What experiences of the Jews in Old Testament times in Jerusalem would be recalled by the ministry of Jesus there?
4. What was the Old Testament background to the dispute about circumcision in the time of the Early Church? Was there any reason why those who supported circumcision for Gentiles should suppose that they were being obedient to Old Testament revelation?
5. Can you suggest why Matthew 1.1–17 and Luke 3.23–38 are described on p. 142 as lists of the ancestors of *Joseph*?

BIBLE

6. For each of the names of the ancestors of Joseph given in Matt. 1.1–17, find a verse in the Old Testament which gives details about the person named. A few of the names do not appear in the Old Testament. Which are these?
7. Examine the New Testament references to Jonah, and describe how the story of this prophet is used by Jesus.

'Jesus Himself knew that all through Israel's history God had been preparing people's hearts and minds for His coming' (p. 147).

In many countries today Christians claim that the traditional religion of the people, like that of the Israelites, has been a preparation for the coming of the Gospel.

In what ways, if any, do you think this is true when, for example: The priest of the sea-god pours a libation among the Ga people of Ghana? When two Brahmin scholars in India discuss the teachings of Hinduism? When spirits are called upon during a voodoo session in the Caribbean? Or when the head of a Tibetan monastery translates the Buddhist scriptures?

DISCUSSION

8. 'The study of Old Testament Theology is a serious waste of time which could better be spent on studying the teachings of the New Testament.' Do you agree? Give reasons for your answer.

9. 'It is more important that we should study the ideas and vocabulary of our own people, than concern ourselves with Israelite ideas and expressions. The traditions of our own country and religion, rather than those of the Old Testament, have been the "preparation" of our people for the coming of Christ and His Church among us.' Do you agree? Give reasons for your answers.

# Key to Study Suggestions

PLEASE NOTE: This key provides information about where the answers can be found. It does not usually provide the answers themselves. Some of the answers are to be found in this textbook, or in its companion volumes on the History of Israel, and the Books of the Old Testament. In these instances the page number, section, paragraph, and lines are given. The paragraph numbers are counted on each page, including the incomplete paragraph at the beginning of some of the pages, but not counting separately headings, or quotations. Other answers may be found by use of a Concordance, Bible dictionary, or Commentary. A good English dictionary is also needed to provide some answers. Suggestions for suitable sources of information are given in these instances. No suggested answers are given where the question depends on local knowledge of the customs or beliefs of people living in the area. Nor are answers usually given where the student is asked to express an opinion on a subject that is open to discussion.

INTRODUCTION: PAGES 5, 6

1. See page 1, para. 4, and page 3, para. 4.
2. Communication, intercourse.
3. See page 2, para. 3, and para. 5—going on to the top of page 3.
4. See page 4, paras. 3 and 4.
5. See page 4, para. 6, and page 5, para. 1.
6. Compare the verses in which 'has revealed' appears, with those in which 'reveals' and 'will reveal' occur. Similarly, compare what is said to have happened because of revelation, with what will happen because of it. The emphasis is upon the future. God is thought of as concerned to maintain and renew His fellowship with men. The past helps, but the future is full of even greater blessings.
7. 7(a) is probably best answered by 7 (b) (iii). But some Christians would not agree.
8. 8(a) (ii) tells us what we should look for as we read the Bible.
   *Exodus 21.15–17* does not give commands that we should follow today, because we believe that death is too heavy a penalty. The law-givers were right to encourage respect for parents, and for human freedom. They had a real insight into the purposes of God in sharing a knowledge of these responsibilities.
   *Amos 9.2–4* expresses the prophet's recognition of God's judgement on evildoers. But we would want to set beside such a passage what Hosea or some other writer has to say about God's mercy. The two ideas are only rightly understood side by side.

*Job 27.1–6* describes Job's anguish at the fact that although he has lived righteously, he has suffered many things. He refuses to accept that he deserves to suffer. As a result, he seems to accuse God of being unjust. We can understand why Job felt as he did, but it is difficult to accept his words either as 'precise theological statements' or as 'promises and prophecies made by God'.

INTRODUCTION: PAGES 10, 11

1. Encouragement, prompting, stimulus.
2. Imaginary, instructive.
3. See page 7, sections 2 and 3.
4. See page 10, lines 6–8, and lines 11–13. Give your own examples.
5. See the section on the message of Ezekiel in Volume 2, pages 72–74.
6. Notice, in particular, the verses where somebody, or some group of people, did *not hearken* to God, or to his messengers.
8. See page 10, lines 19–25.
9. See para. at foot of page 6, and top of page 7.

INTRODUCTION: PAGES 16, 17

1. Knowledge: but the knowledge that comes from a *relationship* with God.
2. God's activity: make known, teach, uncover.
   Men's activity: discover, learn, recognize, understand.
3. See page 14, para. 2, lines 1–9.
4. See page 15, paras 3 and 4.
5. See page 15 final two paras., and page 16 first para.
6. See page 16, lines 14–15.
7. See Deuteronomy 32. 1–43.
8. Use a Concordance to discover this answer.

CHAPTER 1: PAGES 22, 23

1. Your own ideas are important here.
2. Only, sole.
3. See page 18, Section 1, para. 1.
   For JEHOVAH lines 6–11, for YAHWEH lines 3–6, and for the LORD lines 1–3.
4. See page 21, para. 7, lines 1–3, and page 22, para. 1.
5. See page 22, para. 2, lines 4–8.
6. See especially Psalm 115.3–8.
7. See especially Judges 11.24, and Jeremiah 48.13.

CHAPTER 1: PAGES 27, 28

1. To produce.
2. Monotheism.

152

3. (a) See page 24, section 2, para. 2, lines 3–7.
   (b) See page 26, lines 1–2; also Sections 1–6 of this study.
4. See page 9, section 4. Think about the difference between things which are *unexplained*, and those that are *inexplicable*. How do these two ideas affect our understanding of miracles? And of the laws of nature?
5. (a) and (b). Use a Concordance.
6. (a) and (b). Use a Concordance.
7. Read again section 1 on page 24.
8. Read again section 5, which begins on page 26.

## CHAPTER 1: PAGES 31–32

1. Originating.
2. Direction and outcome.
3. See page 29, para. 3, lines 1–4.
4. See page 29, para. 5, lines 3–9.
5. (a) and (b). Use a Concordance.
6. Recall the studies in Vol. 1 of this course.
9. Re-read Vol. 1, Introduction, Section 1.

## CHAPTER 1: PAGES 35, 36

1. Answer (b).
2. Directions.
3. Re-read Sections 1 to 3, on pages 33–4.
5. Law, testimonies, ways, precepts, statutes, commandments, ordinances, word, promise, judgements. Use a good dictionary to explain these terms.
6. Use a Concordance.

## CHAPTER 1: PAGES 40, 41

1. Distinct beings, and separate individuals.
2. Answer (b).
3. The definition implies that Theology is a human activity, 'the attempt to describe'. But God is difficult to describe in human terms. Old Testament writers were unable to grasp and express at all adequately the idea of the Trinity, yet some of their ideas prepared the way for later understanding.
4. See page 39, para. 5, lines 3–7.
5. Notice Isaiah 55.10–11; Psalm 33.6, 9; 2 Kings 3.12.
6. Use a Concordance.
7. Notice what Jesus is recorded as saying at the time of the Last Supper in John 14—17, about his relationship to the Father, and about the Holy Spirit.

8. William Barclay says, 'A great power can exist for years or even centuries without men being able to tap it. The power is there even when men do not know that it is there. . . . The Holy Spirit has always existed; but men never really enjoyed the full power of the Spirit until after Pentecost' (see *The Daily Study Bible: The Gospel of John*, Vol. 1).

## CHAPTER 2: Pages 47, 48

1. Omnipotence—Possessing *all* power.
   Omnipresence—Being available in *all* places.
   Omniscience—Having *all* knowledge.
2. Shows, suggests.
3. See page 44, para. 2, lines 7–11.
4. There are plenty of references to choose from in the section headed 'Angels', pages 44–47.
5. Use a Concordance.
6. If possible, look for a Commentary on the book of Psalms, and see what it has to say about Psalm 82.
8. Part of the answer is to be found in the fact that God is in control of His creation. There are no beings possessing similar authority or power.

## CHAPTER 2: Pages 52, 53

1. Immanence: available, helpful, loving, near, personal.
   Transcendence: almighty, creator, eternal, perfect, separate.
2. Opponent.
3. See page 48, 'The Angel of the Lord', para. 1, lines 1–4.
4. 1 Chronicles 21.1; Job 1 and 2; Zechariah 3.2.
5. Use a Concordance, and restrict your studies to Genesis, Exodus, Leviticus, Numbers, Deuteronomy.
6. Use a Concordance.
7. Christians differ in their answers to this question. Try to understand both both points of view.
8. 'Evil' can be used to mean 'trouble', or 'suffering'.
   Amos believed that trouble was deserved, and sent by God.

## CHAPTER 3: Pages 58, 59

1. Answer (b).
2. His child.
3. Page 56, final 3 lines, and page 58, lines 1–9.
4. (a) See Genesis 1.26–27; 2.7 and 21–22.
   (b) See page 54, para. 3.
5. (a) the king, (b) Jerusalem, (c) sins, (d) One like a son of man. God's authority is greater.
6. Notice specially Genesis 5.3, and any similar verses. Man's relation to God is similar to that of a child to his father.

**CHAPTER 3: PAGES 63, 64**

1. (a) foot, (b) hand, (c) tongue, (d) heart, (e) stomach.
2. Component, and integral.
3. See page 61, para. 5.
4. See page 62, section 2 (i), lines 5 and 6, and page 63, lines 1–3.
5. Use a Concordance, and look at the use of the word *blood* in 2 Samuel.
6. (a) There are six. (b) Imagination, heart (2), soul, mouth, spirit.
   (c) There is no distinct word.
7. See page 59, Man's Nature, para. 1.
8. See page 63, para. 2, lines 1–3.
9. (a) Medical Science is primarily concerned with discovering the physical condition of the patient, and treating physical disorders. But there is plenty of evidence that a person's body, mind, and spirit are inter-related, so that whether we are well or ill, they influence each other. Anger is an emotion, but it has recognizable affects on the physical body. Fear does also. Anxiety can produce headaches and stomach disorders, and exhaustion can cause depression, etc.
   (b) See a dictionary for the meaning of the terms physiology, psychology, psychical research. There are other branches of science which are sub-sections of these three areas of research.

**CHAPTER 3: PAGE 72**

1. Function, and part.
2. *Annihilation:* complete destruction, nothing of a man remains.
   *Reincarnation:* return to earth in a different body, perhaps as a man, or else as an animal or plant.
   *Resurrection:* return to life, either in this world, or in a different world.
   *Survival:* continuing life, away from the body, but perhaps restricted to some earthly place.
   *Translation:* enter heaven, without going through death.
   *Transmigration:* enter another human body at death, perhaps of a child born at the moment of death.
   Evidence is given in this chapter that in biblical times people believed in survival, translation, and resurrection.
3. See page 66, lines 4–7.
4. See whole of section 2, pages 65–68.
5. 'He believed that after death all men enter a place called *Sheol*. There they live an empty, meaningless sort of life, with "no work, or thought, or knowledge" (Ecclesiastes 9.10). Everything that a man has lived for and valued comes to an end (Ecclesiastes 9.5–6).' (Vol. 2, page 123.)
6. It literally means 'destruction', but is used sometimes with the same meaning as Sheol.

**CHAPTER 4: PAGES 77, 78**

1. Ruin.
2. Answer (c).

3. (a) See page 76, lines 4–5.
   (b) See page 76, para. 2, line 2, and para. 4.
4. See page 76, para. 2, lines 7–10.
5. See Psalm 1.1–3, and use a Concordance to find comparable verses by studying such words as *walk, stand, sit.*
6. Psalm 95.9 is a good example. The people tempted (or tested) God. Although they had experienced His goodness they failed to trust Him, and demanded His help because they were afraid He would not give it. Deuteronomy 6.16 warns the people not to behave in this way.

CHAPTER 4: PAGE 84, 85

1. (a) For example: (i) Were you *present* at the funeral? Did you *attend* the funeral? (ii) She gave him a *present* at Christmas. Why don't you *attend* to what I am saying?
2. Rebelliousness, and unkindness ('attitude of mind').
3. *Sin:* See page 79, lines 3–7.
   *Transgression:* See page 79, para. 2, lines 3–5.
4. See page 81, section 4, lines 3–5.
5. See page 81, section 5, para. 2.
6. Hinnom was the name of a valley outside Jerusalem where the people of Israel at times burnt human sacrifices and incense to false gods.
   The physical descriptions of Hell in the New Testament probably had their origins in the horror which Jews felt at the idea of burning human sacrifices. What worse could happen?
7. See section on *God's Wrath*, pages 80–81.
8. (b) See page 82, para. 3.
10. See page 82, para. 3.

CHAPTER 5: PAGES 89, 90

1. Disappointment and frustration.
2. Affection, devotion, sympathy.
3. See page 87, lines 1–4.
4. See page 87, para. 5, lines 2–4, and page 88, paras 2 and 4.
5. See Psalms 23.3; 25.11; 31.3; 79.9; 106.8, etc.
6. Hosea 4.1: kindness.
   Hosea 6.4–6: (v. 4) love; (v. 6) steadfast love.
   Hosea 10.12: steadfast love.
   Hosea 12.6: love.
7. (a) Answer (iii).
   (b) Answer (iii).
8. See page 87, para. 5, lines 6–10.

KEY TO STUDY SUGGESTIONS

CHAPTER 5: PAGES 96, 97

1. Agreement.  2. Answer (b).
3. See page 90, section 1, lines 7–10.
   See page 96, line 4. Give the verbal form of the noun found there.
4. See page 93, section (c), lines 1–21.
5. (a) See Genesis 21.27; 26.28; 31.44.
6. Assyrian Empire: Isaiah 9.7; 16.5; 22.22.
   Babylonian Empire: Jeremiah 33.15, 17; Ezekiel 37.25.
   Persian Empire: Zechariah 6.12–13.
   Greek Empire: Zechariah 12.8.

CHAPTER 5: PAGES 102, 103

1. Dedication and obedience.
2. (a) iv; (b) iii; (c) i; (d) v; (e) ii.
3. See pages 97 and 99, Section 2 (a), (b), and (c).
4. See page 99, section 3.
5. (a) See verses 6, 11, 24, 30, 33, 34.
   (b) Objects used in worship were thought to be unfit for such use if they
       came into contact with people who were ritually unclean. We would
       perhaps want to express things differently, saying that objects only
       become suitable for use in worship when they are known to have been
       set aside for this purpose.
   (c) See verses 3, 5, and 9. One of the goats might have become a sin-
       offering, but was in fact used for another purpose.
   (d) See verses 14, 15, 18, and 19. The life of the animal was considered
       to be in the blood. Possibly the worshippers intended that this gift
       of blood should represent the dedication of their own lives to God.
   (e) See verses 21 and 22.
6. Read again the section on Covenants, with this question in mind. See
   pages 90–96.
7. See page 99, para. 2.
8. See page 101, para. 5, lines 4–17.

CHAPTER 6: PAGES 110, 111

1. Respect and reverence.
2. believing—believable; depending—dependable; having faith—faithful;
   loving—lovable; relying—reliable.
3. (a) The process of writing something from one language in the letters
       used in a different language, which uses a different script.
   (b) Most of the personal names used in English Bibles are transliterations
       from the original Hebrew or Greek.
4. Holiness—fear; faithfulness—trust; loving—love.
5. See page 106, paras. 3 and 4.

6. Explain particularly the words found in these verses, which we have studied in this section: righteousness, truth, believe, steadfast love, and faithfulness.

7. See page 117, para. 4.

8. See entry 'Remnant' in the index of Vol. 2, as well as the section 'The Remnant' on pages 104–105 of this present volume.

9. It is seldom possible to translate a sentence or passage in such a way that it expresses exactly the same ideas as the original. Sentence structures and words are not identical in meaning in different languages. Scholars help by providing as accurate translations as possible, and by writing commentaries in which they explain some of the difficulties. An analytical concordance such as that edited by R. Young and published by the U.S.C.L. helps us to discover the varied ways in which Hebrew and Greek words may be translated.

## CHAPTER 6: PAGES 118, 119

1. Best: friendship. Not possible: antagonism.

2. (a) *Abortion:* the rejection of the foetus from the womb, whether induced or by miscarriage.
    *Euthanasia:* or 'mercy killing'. Death intentionally caused for a patient suffering severe pain, or so severely injured that no normal life can be hoped for.
    *Execution:* Death used as a means of punishment for serious crimes.
    *Manslaughter:* Death caused accidentally, with no prior intention.
    *Murder:* Death caused unlawfully and on purpose.
   (b) The law codes of the Old Testament provide mercy for those guilty of manslaughter, and command execution for some crimes. Abortion, deliberately caused, and euthanasia are not mentioned in the Old Testament, and are subjects of controversy in modern times, even among Christians. The law refers to murder, but there is a debate about what is lawful in God's sight.

3. See page 114, paras. 2–5.

4. See page 117, para. 4.

5. Use a Concordance to discover what Deuteronomy has to say about: the poor, the fatherless, widows, the blind, the lame—all of whom Job helped.

6. See these names in the index to Vol. 1, and the appropriate sections there.

7. These passages are most easily understood if we remember that the Law was intended to make the will of God known to His people. If they rejected it, they were in danger of rejecting God's will. If they clung to the outward significance of the words of the Law they were in danger of misunderstanding His purposes.

8. Certainly inadequate for (c). The prophets, for example, were concerned about more than is stated here.

CHAPTER 7: PAGES 123, 124

1. Answer (b).
2. Desire, dream, and optimism.
3. See page 120, para. 2.
4. See page 121, paras. 3 and 4.
5. God's living, active, and personal relationship with His people is the basis of His work of salvation in these chapters. Their response will prepare the way for others to be blessed.
6. See Vol. 2, pages 130–131.
7. Romans 8.18–38 will help here.
8. Deutero–Isaiah expresses far more openly, and with more reason for confidence, the writer's assurance that God is about to save His people.

CHAPTER 7: PAGES 130, 131

1. See Psalms 96.6; 104.1; 145.5.
2. Rule.
3. See Vol. 2, pages 55–7.
4. Given an important place in the hearts and lives of his people.
5. See Vol. 2, pages 58 and 60.

CHAPTER 8: PAGES 141, 142

1. Digested.
2. Answer (b).
3. See page 135, final two lines, and page 136, first two lines. Jesus taught in Aramaic, and used the Hebrew Scriptures. The Gospel writers took account of this, e.g. Matthew 27.46.
4. See page 137, paras. 2–4.
5. Matthew took literally what was intended as a poetic parallelism in Zechariah. Perhaps the Septuagint version influenced his understanding of this verse?
6. For example: Romans 1.20; Psalm 19.1–4.
7. See page 140, section 5, lines 3–5.
8. The letter to the Philippians was a personal message to Paul's friends, to say 'thank you' for a gift they had sent to him while he was in prison. It is not chiefly concerned to present the Gospel in theological terms, nor does it attempt to answer questions that would need the kind of instruction that would naturally involve quotations from the Jewish scriptures.

CHAPTER 8: PAGES 147–149

1. Subjects.
2. Answer (a).
3. See the references to Jerusalem in the subject index of Vol. 1.

KEY TO STUDY SUGGESTIONS

4. See page 144, para. 5.

5. Joseph was not the natural father of Jesus. He was only his guardian, and husband of Mary. Jesus was not a descendant in the normal sense of the people in these lists. He did inherit the responsibility for spiritual leadership in Israel which had been held by some of these people. He was adopted into this family.

6. Use a Concordance to discover the verses. The names not found in the Old Testament come towards the end of the list, and may derive from lists of immediate ancestors preserved by the family of Joseph.

7. Use a Concordance. In some English versions of the New Testament the Greek form of the name is used: Jonas.

# Bible Reference Index

# Subject Index

173

SUBJECT INDEX

LORD, The, 18
'Lord's anointed', the, 127, 143
Love, 87, 88, 90, 91, 105, 107, 109
Loyalty, 117, 118

Man, destiny of, 1; nature of, 1, 47, 54, 56, 58–63, 71, 74, 76, 86; role in life, 65, 66
Marriage, 114
Mediums, 44
Mercy, God's, 104
Messenger of God, 10
Messiah, 94, 95, 127
Micah, 104, 127
Miracles, 26
Monotheism, 34
Morality, 32, 35, 112
Moses, 7, 21, 66, 68, 80, 92, 93, 126, 127, 141, 143
Musicians, 68

Nation, 88, 97
Natural order, 24, 25, 26, 55
Nehemiah, 95
New age, 124
New community, 101, 125
New covenant, 95, 96, 141
New Testament writers, 36, 37, 143
Noah, 86, 92, 143

Obedience, 30, 34, 35, 73, 93, 95, 99, 101
Old Testament, the, as God's Truth, 12; as God's Word, 2, 4, 5; theology of, 33, 138; value of, 1, 3
Omnipotence, 24
'One who will come', the, 125, 126, 136
Order, 24, 25

P-Tradition, 24, 55, 56, 58, 94
Parallelism, 88
Patriarchs, 14, 19, 24, 68, 69, 93
Paul, 138, 140
Peace, 31; peace offering, 99
People of God, 15; People of Israel, 34
Persians, 23
'Persons', 37
Physical nature of man, 60
Polygamy, 114
Phylacteries, iv, 18, 145

Polytheism, 33
Power, 39
Praise, 110
Presence of God, 26, 42
Priests, 10, 68
Promise, 125
Prophecy, 125, 136
Prophets, 3, 10, 68, 81, 126, 127, 137, 138; Prophetic hope, 121, 125
Psalms, 138; Psalmists, 3
Punishment, 73, 80, 82, 86, 101
Purposes, God's, 1, 4, 10, 12, 15

Quotations from the OT, use of, 135, 136, 138, 139, 141

Re-creation, 90, 91
Rejoicing, 110
Relationships, between God and man, 55, 58, 87, 88, 90, 92, 95–97, 99, 105; between human beings, 111
Religion, 33, 34
Remnant, the, 104, 105, 129, 140
Repentance, 73, 74
Respect for life, 112
Response to God, 30, 31, 99, 101, 109, 116
Restitution, 100
Resurrection, 71
Revelation, God's, of Himself, 4, 11, 12, 13, 15, 88, 105, 106, 129, 145; through Jesus, 5, 137, 148; in the NT, 137, 148
Righteous, the, 77, 79, 82, 117, 120, 124, 125, 129
Righteousness, 31, 34, 106, 112, 117

Sabbath, 94, 144
Sacrifice, 35, 42, 44, 97–101, 145
Saints, 129
Salvation, 86, 90, 92, 101, 104 ,105, 120, 121, 125, 140
Samaria, 144
Samuel, 10
Satan, 46, 49, 52, 76
Scripture, as God's Word, 1, 137
Separation from God, 77
Septuagint, 135, 136
Seraphim, 45
Servant', the, 101, 129

175